# REGIONAL DYNAMICS

# REGIONAL DYNAMICS

*The Basis of Electoral Support in Britain*

## WILLIAM H. FIELD

*Georgian Court College, Lakewood NJ, USA*

FRANK CASS
LONDON • PORTLAND, OR

*First Published in 1997 in Great Britain by*
FRANK CASS PUBLISHERS
Newbury House, 900 Eastern Avenue
London, IG2 7HH

*and in the United States of America by*
FRANK CASS PUBLISHERS
c/o ISBS, 5804 N.E. Hassalo Street
Portland, Oregon, 97213-3644

*Website:* http://www.frankcass.com

Copyright © 1997 William H. Field

British Library Cataloguing in Publication Data

Field, William H.
  Regional dynamics : the basis of electoral support in Britain
  1. Voting research – Great Britain – History – 20th century
  2. Great Britain – Politics and government – 20th century
  I. Title
  324.9'41'08

ISBN 0-7146-4782-9 (cloth)
ISBN 0-7146-4336-X (paper)

Library of Congress Cataloging-in-Publication Data

Field, William H.
  Regional dynamics : the basis of electoral support in Britain /
William H. Field.
    p. cm.
  Includes bibliographical references and index.
  ISBN 0-7146-4782-9. — ISBN 0-7146-4336-X (pbk)
  1. Great Britain—Economic conditions—Regional disparities.
  2. Great Britain—Economic conditions—1945–1993.  3. Great Britain—
  Politics and government—1979–  4. Elections—Great Britain.
  5. Dependency. I. Title.
  HC256.6.F54  1997
  330.941–dc21                                                97–1303
                                                                 CIP

Printed in Great Britain by
Bookcraft (Bath) Ltd, Midsomer Norton, Avon

# Contents

List of Tables                                                          vi

List of Figures                                                        vii

Foreword by Vernon Bogdanor                                             ix

Acknowledgments                                                         xi

Chapter One: Introduction                                               1

Chapter Two: The Electoral Geography of Britain,
1885–1992                                                               27

Chapter Three: Current Explanations for
Regional Change: A Critical Evaluation                                  64

Chapter Four: The Core–Periphery Cleavage:
Concepts and Interpretations                                           78

Chapter Five: A Dynamic Model of Core and Periphery                   100

Chapter Six: Stability in Change in British Politics                  166

Postscript: The 1997 General Election in the Context
of the Core–Periphery Continuum                                       183

Appendix: Data Sources and Expansions                                 189

Bibliography                                                          195

Index                                                                205

# Tables

Table 3.1 Distribution of the Economically
Active and Employed Population by Occupational
Category, 1951–91                                                    67

Table 3.2 Patterns and Components of Regional
Voting, 1979–87                                                      70

Table 5.1 Geographic Origins of Members of the
House of Commons in Great Britain                                   134

Table 5.2 Explaining the Conservative Vote,
January 1910                                                        160

Table 5.3 Comparing Dynamic Models: 1922                            161

Table 5.4 Comparing Dynamic Models: 1951                            162

Table 5.5 Comparing Dynamic Models: 1992                            162

Table A1 Eigenvalues for Principle Components
Extraction on Core–Periphery Variables                              194

# Figures

Figure 2.1 Conservative Strength in North and South,
1885–December 1910                                      37

Figure 2.2 Conservative Strength in North and South,
1955–92                                                 47

Figure 2.3 Inter-election Stability                     51

Figure 2.4 Geographic Stability of Conservative and
Unionist Party Support                                  54

Figure 2.5 Differences in Party Support between
North and South                                         56

Figure 2.6 Conservative (Conservative/Unionist)
Electoral Support                                       59

Figure 4.1 Attitudes towards Government Power,
1970 and 1987                                           84

Figure 4.2 Core and Periphery: A Static Model           91

Figure 5.1 Sheep per Acre of Agricultural Land by
County Relative to National Sheep Population
Density                                               110–13

Figure 5.2 Concentration of Corporate Head Offices:
Ratio of Percentage of National Offices in County to
Percentage of National Population in County           118–21

Figure 5.3 Concentration of Newspaper Titles:
Ratio of Percentage of Titles in County to Percentage
of Population in County                                    124–7

Figure 5.4 Concentration of Political Élites: Ratio of
Percentage of MPs with Origins in County to
Population in County                                       130–3

Figure 5.5 Population Migration, Relative to National
Gain/Loss                                                 136–9

Figure 5.6 Railway Service: Stations per Square Mile
Relative to National Density                              144–7

Figure 5.7 Core and Periphery in 1891, 1921, 1951
and 1991                                                  154–7

# Foreword

by Vernon Bogdanor
(Professor of Government, Oxford University)

THIS IS a pioneering book. Many have noticed the 'north–south divide' in British politics: indeed they have built their academic reputations on seeking to explain it. William Field, however, is the first to notice that this divide marks the resurgence of a core–periphery cleavage which was also dominant in British politics in the years before 1914. He shows how astonishingly similar the geographical pattern of the vote was in the general election of 1987 to that in the two general elections of 1910, the last before the outbreak of the First World War. Many of the same constitional issues – devolution and reform of the second chamber – were coming to the fore then as now, symbolic perhaps of the desire of the periphery to attain equality with the core.

Thirty years ago, S. M. Lipset and Stein Rokkan identified the stability of voting patterns as characteristic of the advanced industrial societies of Western Europe. William Field is the first to apply the Lipset/Rokkan model to British politics in detail, and the first also to notice and analyse the profound *historicity* of voting patterns in Britain. This historicity itself gives rise to fascinating questions. Are we now seeing the resurgence of a pattern which, from the end of the First World War to the 1980s, was submerged by the politics of class? Is the decline of class leading to the resurrection of older cleavages – and if so what are the consequences for British politics? Was 'Thatcherism', so dominant in British politics in the 1980s, more a *consequence* of profound social and geographical changes than a *cause*, and were these changes not laying the ground for a new individualism, strong in the dominant core but weak in the periphery?

Fundamental questions arise, in particular, for the parties of the Left. The stronghold of the parties has always lain in the periphery, and this is a large part of the explanation of why they have so often been in opposition. Before the First World War, however, the Liberals and the young Labour Party succeeded in breaking the grip of Conservative dominance by means of an electoral pact – the Gladstone–MacDonald pact of 1903. Indeed, by the time of the two elections of 1910, such was the strength of co-operation between the two parties of the Left that there could be said to be a Progressive hegemony in British politics. The years before the First World War were in fact far more likely to herald the strange death of Conservative than of Liberal England. During the 1980s, by contrast, and indeed, until 1997, the politics of the Left was marked by division rather than co-operation, although there are signs that this period of division may be coming to an end.

'I never make predictions', film producer Sam Goldwyn once said, 'especially about the future.' William Field is no more able than any other student of politics to predict the future. What he can do, however, is to make sense of the past. The central message of his book is that we must peer much further back into the past if we are fully to understand British electoral behaviour. Field brings to his analysis a deep knowledge and understanding of statistics and a rigour not always found in historical analysis. It is not surprising that the thesis on which *Regional Dynamics* is based was awarded the Samuel H. Beer Dissertation Prize by the British Politics Group of the American Political Science Association for the best thesis on British politics produced in 1995.

Historians, Benedetto Croce once said, imagine the past and remember the future. In analysing the past, William Field offers us a key to the future. Indeed time future, as T. S. Eliot noticed, is itself 'contained in time past'. It is precisely because it succeeds in making sense of the past that *Regional Dynamics* offers us the best guide we are likely to have as to what the future will be like.

# Acknowledgments

VERNON BOGDANOR asked me an interesting question when I was a visiting student at Nuffield College in 1991. He was curious about whether the expanding 'north–south divide' could be seen as the result of a weakening of the class cleavage and the re-emergence of older core–periphery differences. The initial answer was published in *Electoral Studies* in 1993; this work represents a much more complete answer. The search took me through lengthy volumes of British history, eyestrain from staring at a computer, several transatlantic journeys, and occasional bouts of disbelief that the question *had* any answer at all.

That I did find an answer is due in no small part to Vernon's encouragement. Thanks are also due to Pippa Norris, with whom I had frequent discussions, and who read every chapter more times than she would care to admit. Among other individuals who have provided assistance or support Sid Milkis, Spencer Wellhofer, Jim Hollifield, Jim Alt, David Butler, Dan Tichenor, and Steven Burg deserve accolades for their critical interventions at decisive points. The members of the British Politics Seminar at Harvard University's Center for European Studies offered helpful advice at an early stage of this investigation. While all the people I have mentioned influenced the outcome of this project, I alone bear responsibility for any errors.

A large amount of data was evaluated in preparing this work. Along with the ESRC, who granted access to data held in their archive, Ken Wald gave me access to his records while David Paul of the Government Documents Division of the Harvard University Library System was extremely diligent in tracking down unusual sources. Pippa Norris and Joni Lovenduski provided me with a copy of the British Candidate

Study. John Yeboah, of Clark University, spent more time than he had available developing the map outlines for the pre-1974 county boundaries. I am grateful to Brandeis University and Nuffield College, Oxford, for shelter during research and writing. Finally, while I mention her last, Susan Field provided more support and critical analysis than everyone else combined. With apologies for my mood swings and gratitude for their love, I would like to dedicate this volume to her and our two children.

# CHAPTER ONE

# Introduction

GREAT BRITAIN'S political cohesion is breaking down. In the 1950s electoral outcomes could be predicted on the basis of a few seats and a national swing; today, different regions in the country have moved disproportionately to support one party or another. The Conservatives won 43 per cent of the northern seats in the 1955 election but only 26 per cent in 1992. In the south, excluding Devon and Cornwall, their share of seats rose from 62 per cent to 74 per cent.

The increasingly pronounced division of Britain into two distinct voting blocs, each with its own distinct electorates, problems, attitudes, and goals, reflects the renewed importance of the core–periphery cleavage in the country. In the 1980s the most important problem in the north of England and Scotland was unemployment; this contrasts with the main problem in the south-east which was how to control rapid economic growth and its attendant transportation and communication problems.[1] During these years the Conservatives seemed unable, or at best unwilling, to comprehend the severity of northern employment problems. Speaking in 1985, the Secretary of State for Trade and Industry, Lord Young, rejected the need for intervening in the north:

> There was more industrialisation in the north, originally, therefore there now has to be more de-industrialisation. Until 70 years ago the north was always the richest part of the country. The two present growth industries – the City and tourism – are concentrated in the south. I try to

encourage people to go north; that is where all the great country houses are because that's where the wealth was. Now some of it is in the south. It's our turn, that's all.[2]

In the run-up to the 1992 election campaign, Labour's shadow budget gave the Conservatives considerable leverage with which to sway those critical 'C2s' (skilled manual workers) who lived more in the south-east than elsewhere.[3] In 1992 Labour's failure to pick up such critical seats as Battersea in London, and Basildon and Corby elsewhere in the south-east, any of which would have fallen had the local change in vote matched the national swing of 2.6 per cent, highlights the problems each party had in gaining support outside its heartland. Despite the economic failings of the Conservative government and the general perception that the Conservatives had run out of ideas, not enough 'Essex men' could bring themselves to vote Labour. Differences in attitudes on issues played a part in the electoral division,[4] but issue differences tend to reflect more fundamental differences in political outlook and philosophy.

Politically, the reappearance of regional differences in Britain raises the possibility of the end of Britain as a single political entity, and the secession of Scotland within the larger framework of the European Union. The success of the Scottish Nationalists (SNP) at all elections since 1974 has challenged the political viability of Britain. While the break-up of Britain may seem less likely following the Conservative Party's relative success in Scotland in the 1992 general election, issues of proportional representation, devolution and the possibility of an independent Scotland have been highly visible since at least the mid-1970s. While cultural differences may not seem as difficult to resolve as they are in Canada or Belgium, both countries could point the way for a future break-up of Britain along lines that reflect the electoral divisions of the 1980s.

Observers have called this phenomenon of dissimilar levels of regional party support the new 'north–south divide' and have built an academic industry trying to explain it.[5] Far from being new, however, the divide bears striking resemblance to the distribution of party support in Edwardian times, especially in the general elections of 1910, when core–periphery issues dominated the political debate. This book argues that the contemporary geographical distribution of support marks the resurgence of a dormant core–periphery cleavage which has had major consequences for the British party system.

The new north–south divide is not precisely the same as the old core–periphery cleavage, of course. The cleavage that separated Liberals and Conservatives in the late nineteenth century is generally considered to have been of a religious character;[6] religion is hardly the defining characteristic of British politics today but there are striking similarities in other respects: the economic structures of the north of England, Wales, and Scotland retain the economic characteristics of large industrial enterprises with unionised workers, while the south retains its ability to suck money into the City and to generate well-paid service jobs to support the financial sector. Furthermore, many of the same political arguments about Scottish and Welsh devolution that were mooted before the outbreak of the First World War are being again raised after a long hiatus. Finally, the present electoral geography of British politics is very similar to that in 1910, when the Conservative Party dominated seats south of a line running horizontally across England from the northern end of the English–Welsh border and anti-Conservative parties dominated elsewhere.[7]

There is one central question that guides this study: *is the north–south divide a recreation and permutation of an earlier, core–periphery divide, or is it an unrelated phenomenon whose origins must be traced to other factors?* The following pages present results of an investigation that shed some light on this question. If the contemporary north–south divide is indeed a repetition of an earlier phenomenon, parties can use this knowledge to shape their election strategies to make best use of the factors that once again underpin British politics. Election results suggest that nationalism in Wales and Scotland has become a serious threat to the integrity of the United Kingdom, much as Irish nationalism altered the boundaries of the country in 1922. If, on the other hand, the election results are not related to issues of core and periphery, then nationalism can be seen as more of a passing fad than a serious element in Britain's political debate. One answer raises the possibility of the break-up of Britain; the other provides reassurance that the British polity is indeed sound and not on the brink of substantial alteration or perhaps even disintegration.

## THEORETICAL OVERVIEWS

There are two major explanatory frameworks that have been developed to explain voting behaviour. *Social identity* explanations, based on the Michigan model of socialisation, posit that individuals vote according to a highly stable identification with a specific party. In this model, an individual's electoral stance is an integral part of that person's identity: as W. S. Gilbert remarked in *Iolanthe*, every person born is 'either a little Liberal or else a little Conservative.' The argument suggests that partisan identification is developed primarily through group attachments and familial associations, and an individual's tendency to vote for a particular party does not generally change over time. Voting is an act of affirmation of membership in a political group. As a result, the typical voter 'knows little about politics, is not interested in politics, does not participate in politics, does not organise his or her political attitudes in a coherent manner, and does not think in structured, ideological terms.'[8] Because voter loyalties are driven by group membership, and groups are part of the institutional structure of society, this approach is also known as the *institutional* or *social psychological* model of voting.

A natural extension from the individual voter's stability associated with the social identity model is aggregate geographic stability in electoral support. If residents of a particular area make their electoral choice as an affirmation of group membership, then, barring a major disruption such as a partisan realignment or massive migration, the area should show a stable level of support for the major competing parties.

The 1970s and 1980s have seen an apparent decline in voter constancy throughout Europe and North America.[9] Voter volatility appears to have increased, and the electorate shows signs of partisan dealignment, where people are no longer defining their social identity as clearly in terms of party attachment. This has reduced the persuasiveness of the social identity model and has led to an increased interest in models that see voting as instrumental rather than affirmative. *Rational* theories suppose that voters decide how to vote primarily on the basis of their perceived interests. Interests are generally defined in terms of economic well-being, so the rational or economic model of voting interprets elections on the basis of individual evaluations of the merits of the economic programmes offered by the competing parties. An alteration in the geography of the vote would tend to reflect a new distribution of interests or geographically polarised perceptions of the government's economic policies.

The theory of economic voting lies behind the speech by Lord Young quoted above. The theory also lies behind much current research on the north–south divide. Several studies have tested various economic explanations for this divide. *Objective* economic conditions, defined as changes in such indicators as unemployment rates, interest rates and the inflation level, and measured at the constituency, regional or national level, have been found to relate to voting outcomes,[10] but there is little consistency about the strength of the relationship from election to election. Aside from a few general comments about Conservative electoral success in recent elections loosely reflecting middle-class economic success, the studies have failed to demonstrate a strong association between particular economic phenomena and voting.

*Subjective* economic conditions, defined as how individuals claim to feel about their personal financial situation and future prospects, pose even more of a problem. The attitude of a voter evaluating the past performance of the government varies in part according to that individual's predisposition toward the party in government. The same is true for any evaluation of future prospects, where voters judge the likelihood of their personal economic situation improving or worsening as a result of government action. Low inflation, low unemployment, rising wages, rising house prices, low interest rates for borrowers, high rates for savers, higher government spending on particular projects, and lower overall spending cannot all occur simultaneously. While the general public might want 'full employment, larger pay packets, stable prices, ... a strong currency and balanced international payments'[11] at the actual time of evaluation, different voters, predisposed to favour different parties, tend to interpret economic conditions in ways that reinforce their party predisposition.

## Synthesis and extension

Neither the social identity model nor the economic model is adequate in its own right; neither explains electoral developments completely. Voters are not as locked into their preferences as the social identity model assumes, yet people are neither so fickle nor so well-informed as to constantly re-evaluate their partisan preferences in light of changing political events. The approach developed in these pages combines the two alternatives into a social identity model, influenced by long-term trends in society's economic and social structures. Examining British electoral politics through the lens of this model provides a more theoretically and historically grounded explanation for the emergence of the north–south divide. It relates contemporary voting patterns to the great Liberal–Conservative debates in the late nineteenth century. Perhaps most important in terms of policy implications and electoral strategies, the interpretation offered here creates a framework for exploring current electoral debates and the role of the Conservative Party in the coming years.

The utility of this approach lies in its focus on the contemporary implications of the historical development of the British party system. The origins of partisan support today lie in the structures that have emerged reflecting the economic and social organisations of Britain. Class, religion, race, and ethnicity are simply the most obvious of these divisive societal features that structure group conflict. These features divide the electorate. Following the appearance of democratic conflict, group membership placed individuals on one side or another of the resulting cleavages. Parties aligned themselves along the same cleavage lines; group membership, therefore, exerts a powerful influence on the vote.

*Cleavages, geography and party support*
A cleavage is a division of individuals or organisations between whom there is some possibility of conflict. A cleavage is thus a precondition of, but not an indicator for, conflict. Cleavages occur in society and in party systems. It is useful to label each type as *societal* cleavages and *party-system* cleavages respectively. In the social identity model, and in the approach developed here, societal cleavages are seen to influence party-system cleavages and therefore to form the basis of individual vote choices.

Cleavages provide an important conceptual tool for understanding the apparently chaotic nature of elections, campaigns, and the origins of popular support for government action. Within the social identity model, cleavages provide an underlying structural or institutional framework on which the policy options of the day can be laid. They also give a guide for exploring the origins and current bases of party organisation. The concept of the cleavage enables us to more easily understand the issues and socio-economic characteristics that divide electorates, bring parties together and make government possible.

Political parties are intermediaries between societal cleavages and government action. As such, party-system cleavages should reflect societal cleavages and should, in turn, affect the structure of conflict within the government administration.[12] The study of party-system cleavages, therefore, is useful both for its contribution towards an understanding of the fundamental structures of society and in exploring the effects of change on the political arena.

Stein Rokkan developed a model that related societal cleavages to party-system cleavages. The Rokkan model of the historical development of western Europe suggests that four overriding cleavages structure the party systems as a result of the revolutions inherent in European nation-building.[13] Two result from the national revolutions as the central nation-building élites came into conflict with peripheral cultures and with the power and privileges of the church. The others derive from the industrial revolution: landed interests versus industrial/urban interests and employers versus workers. These cleavages played a fundamental role in European political history: in Britain and elsewhere, parties mobilised electorates along these cleavage lines, and, once mobilised by a party representing one side of a cleavage, voters developed a loyalty to that party at the expense of alternative party attachments. As a result of this process, the balance of electoral power in any historical period resulted from the distribution of the voting populations across all the important cleavages up to that time. In an observation which has come to be known as the freezing hypothesis, Rokkan posited that contemporary European party systems reflect the societal cleavages of the 1920s and that, while these societal cleavages may well have become less divisive, the party-system cleavages that were mobilised around them continue to structure most European political arenas:

> The most important of the party alternatives got set for each national citizenry during the phases of mobilization just before or just after the final extension of the suffrage and have remained roughly the same through decades of subsequent changes in the structural conditions of partisan choice.[14]

The majority of the cleavages Rokkan lists need little explanation. The church–state cleavage pits parties with a religious base against parties with a secular, even anti-clerical, ideology. This party-system cleavage results from debates over control of education and the extent to which religious law can be applied to non-religious occasions. A prime example here is the struggle in France between the Catholic Church and the Jacobin state over the extent to which religious schools could be independent from, yet supported by, the state.[15] A similar cleavage has divided the Christian Democrats from the strictly secular Socialists and Communists in Italy.

The land–capital cleavage is expressed in France in the struggle between farmers and urban areas over the price for food, a struggle which nearly derailed the Uruguay Round of the GATT. The party-system aspect of this cleavage has weakened somewhat in the largest European democracies but it remains strong in several Scandinavian countries.

The class cleavage needs the least explanation as it has been the focus of most scholarly work on political parties and social structures in Europe and is the most long-standing and important phenomenon in the politics of most European democracies. In the societal sphere, trade unions combat owners' federations in Germany, France, Britain, and elsewhere over the distribution of wealth. This struggle is reflected in party systems which pit the Left against the Right in struggles for control over the elected government.

The final cleavage of the four is harder to explain as it results from a more amorphous contest over power and social organisation rather than something explicit such as wages, prices, or religious influence. In the Rokkan typology, the cleavage pits the nation-building élites of the central government against the older, local élites of the more distant provinces. Also at odds are cultural norms and the power to impose them, traditions, and perhaps even language usage. Core and periphery are firmly rooted in the fundamental economic structures of society in so far as these reflect long-standing social networks and the distribution of power.[16]

The definition of a model of the core–periphery cleavage, and the explanation of its impact over time, form the centre-piece of this study. Surprisingly, most work on core–periphery relations has not included a specifically territorial dimension; in a review article, Spencer Wellhofer complains that, while 'this usage [of core and periphery] has gained a spatial or territorial dimension ... it is seldom explicit and the spatial parameters are rarely incorporated into the discussion.'[17] This book attempts to correct the omission.

The electoral map of Britain shows considerable variation in the regional pattern of the vote. This pattern seems to relate to regional loyalties and sectional interests. The pattern suggests the periodic emergence of a core–periphery cleavage. However, the definition of core and periphery must be made independent of electoral outcomes or the diagnosis of core–periphery influence can offer no explanation of those outcomes. Definitions of core and periphery should be based on long-term historical processes, such as the expansion of state authority, or on socio-economic consequences of a division of labour between regions in a country, but not on short-term political events such as election returns, parliamentary divisions, or the salience of particular political issues. These three sets of events are dependent rather than independent variables. History influences contemporary events; the present does not influence the past (though it may affect our understanding of it). While government action can influence societal cleavages by creating an institutional structure favourable to one group rather than another, or by encouraging supra-group identities, societal cleavages generally predate and condition government divisions and party-system cleavages.

## BRITAIN AND THE ROKKAN TYPOLOGY

The historical development of the British political economy fits well with the Rokkan typology. The expanding monarchy came into conflict first with local power centres in the periphery and then with the independent power structure of the Catholic Church. Later, conflict over the allocation of wealth and privileges erupted between agrarian and urban interests, and were fought out in the Corn Laws debates of the 1830s. As the franchise spread to lower and lower members of the social hierarchy, new voters mobilised around the existing cleavages. With the gradual spread of democracy, the struggle over the control of the state focused on the dispute between free-trading industrialists and protectionist agricultural élites. The political mobilisation of the industrial workforce created the last cleavage. After the arrival of universal suffrage, there were no more new voters to mobilise around new cleavages, so 'the party systems of the 1960s reflect, with few but significant exceptions, the cleavage structure of the 1920s'.[18]

### Britain: a poor fit?

Rokkan limited himself to stating that historical events

suggested the presence of a core–periphery cleavage, mentioning the type of political conflict that could take place across the boundary but declining to specify the economic, social, or cultural parameters of that cleavage. The area of contention between core and periphery groups lies in the realm of political, social, economic, and possibly religious control. More specifically, the core wishes to expand its power over surrounding regions and communities while people in the periphery strive to maintain their independence from core control. The debate is centred around who exercises power. The conflict may thus involve the degree of independence exercised by local government, small company against expansive conglomerate, or community-based religion against state-sponsored and centrally organised religious structures.

The presence of these types of conflict may be indicative of the existence of a core–periphery cleavage. If a core–periphery cleavage exists, the Rokkan thesis suggests political parties would have formed to mobilise support on either side of it. Thus, a regional basis to political parties, or the polarisation of a country into regionally based political movements, would reflect that cleavage. Furthermore, given the freezing hypothesis, this regionalism should be relatively constant over time. The problem that we face when examining Great Britain is one of change rather than constancy. Bill Miller documented how the national (England versus Scotland versus Wales) swings changed over time, giving Scotland anti-Conservative tendencies in the last years of the nineteenth century that disappeared in the middle of this century, only to reappear to a greater or lesser extent since 1970.[19] British electoral politics do not appear to fit the freezing hypothesis when examined on a geographic basis. Despite the findings of several cross-national studies that suggest either that the freezing hypothesis is no longer correct or that it remains in force, little analysis has been performed on how regional fluctuations in party support relate to this hypothesis. Of those studies that have been published, the time span is too limited to trace the contemporary geography of the vote back to the period when the party system initially froze.[20]

Not only have the geographical dimensions of party support changed over the years; so, too, has the salience of core–periphery or regional issues. Religious differences have affected British politics since before the Glorious Revolution of 1688. Mary, Queen of Scots, was deposed and beheaded in 1587 because her Catholic faith threatened the religious and political survival of the English Reformation. Even earlier, Queen Mary I, half sister of Queen Elizabeth I, caused the shedding of much blood, although not her own, over the issue of whether Protestantism or Catholicism would be the state religion in any part of Britain. In the seventeenth century, religious persecution drove many Puritans and Quakers out of Britain, first to the Netherlands, then to the New World. Of the Dissenters who stayed in Britain, most were in the periphery (namely Wales, northern England, Scotland, Devon, and Cornwall).

Growing up as a Nonconformist in the nineteenth century was very different from growing up in the Anglican Church. The whole moral ethic was far more rigid than in the Established Church. Nonconformity insisted 'upon the authority of moral principles in all matters of public policy.'[21] Anglican intolerance in politics was matched, if not exceeded, by Nonconformist intolerance in morals. By the end of the nineteenth century, when the Liberal and Conservative parties came into mass existence, they organised around these deep, pre-existing religious cleavages. From this alignment springs Macaulay's mid-nineteenth century description of the Anglican Church as 'the Tory party at prayer' and Gladstone's characterisation of the religious vitality and political strength of the many Nonconformist sects as 'the backbone of British Liberalism'.[22] Differences between church and chapel were indeed great, and the electoral map reflected the religious map.

Religion was a powerful and divisive element in late Victorian and Edwardian politics; with the Anglican Church so inextricably bound up with the English Crown, religious conflict was in its essence a manifestation of the core–periphery cleavage. There was a clash over the 'authority of moral principles', but the real debate was not over the presence or absence of religion in people's lives, as with the contention between the Christian Democrats and the Radicals, Socialists, and Communists in France and Germany. Liberals divided from Conservatives over the role that the established, state-sponsored church should play in the affairs of people who were members of other churches. Liberals wanted the freedom to pursue their own version of religious salvation. The issues in contention revolved around control: funding for education, recognition of marriage rites, access to a university education, and freedom of religion.

The Church of England was loath to permit a reduction in the power of its privileged place in British and Irish society – witness Sir Robert Peel's placing of 'Ireland and Repeal agitation' at the top of a list of troubles in a letter to the Governor-General of India in 1842[23] – but Anglican, and therefore Crown, intolerance of Dissenters did decline slowly. The first step toward emancipation was in 1828 with the repeal of the Test and Corporation Acts; later steps included the repeal of the Catholic Tithing Tax in 1838, Irish Disestablishment in 1869–71, the introduction of state funding for non-Anglican church schools in 1897, the granting to local councils of authority over non-sectarian schools in 1902, Welsh disestablishment in 1920, and finally the creation of the Irish Free State in 1922. The majority of these policies were passed by Liberal governments returning power to local structures.

With the passing of the Edwardian Age and the political emancipation that followed the First World War, religion and regionalism seemed to pass from the scene, or at the least to become much less salient. A major reason for this was the expansion of the franchise in 1918 that overwhelmed the older partisan loyalties and cleavage structures.[24] The class cleavage replaced them and froze: the Labour/Conservative debate over the power of the working classes versus the privileges of the owners and the bourgeoisie became the main issue. Any regional differences in party support could easily be attributed to differences in the power and organisation of the working class, or the lingering effects of prior historical experiences that confounded rational explanation.[25]

The time when the entire nation would swing in the same political direction has passed. There has been considerable discussion of a new regional basis to British politics. Electorally and in terms of the political issues raised in and out of Parliament, 'region' and 'nation' have regained a share of the spotlight. From the referendums on Scottish and Welsh devolution in 1979 to the renewed emphasis on the Welsh language in Wales, to the emergence of a pro-devolution platform in the 1992 Labour party manifesto, a considerable part of British political debate since the 1970s has occurred in the context of a growing sensitivity toward regional differences. To feed this debate, nationalist parties advocating independence in Scotland and the preservation of a language identity in Wales have captured substantial shares of the vote in those nations. Core–periphery politics are back.

## Hypotheses for Britain

What, if anything, caused the disappearance of core–periphery conflict from the British political scene earlier this century, and what has led to its re-emergence? While there is a considerable interplay between election results and issues raised by the parties, the two do not exist in a vacuum. Rather, the political arena exists concurrently with, and to a great extent in a subservient status to, the economic and social arenas. Politics reflects economic and social realities to a great extent.

How, then, can one account for the re-emergence of the north–south divide? The main argument in the following chapters is that *the core–periphery cleavage in the socio-economic structure of British society has re-emerged since the mid-1960s and the political cleavage has simply mirrored it.* The other explanations for voting stability and change play a role in our understanding of electoral dynamics but they are insufficient in and of themselves.

Economic and socialisation theories are naturally part of the explanation of British politics; many individuals do vote on the basis of how their parents voted and on the basis of how they feel the various parties will fare in dealing with the many problems of government. But that is not the only basis for electoral choice, nor indeed the primary basis. Cleavage structures provide a fundamental lens through which voters evaluate electoral choices. Dramatic changes in voting patterns can be traced in part to changes in the salience of cleavage structures, whether those changes result from changes in the electorate (such as an extension of the franchise) or the rise of new cleavages. By placing the voting act within an institutional structure, core–periphery analysis gives an overall framework within which an observer can make sense of group and individual actions.

Core and periphery have socio-economic meaning as well as political meaning. To show that core and periphery were important at the beginning of the period under study in these pages, that they declined in importance and then re-emerged, it is necessary to show that the economic and social conditions of core and periphery existed, declined, and re-emerged. It is not adequate to stay in the political arena and explain elections in terms of issues, and issues in terms of elections.

Political conflict generally reflects social and economic divisions in society. To a great extent, political cleavages depend on these divisions for long-term expression. Just as the objective conditions that engender mass unionisation, worker unrest, and political mobilisation of class interests require the human element to organise and lead, so too do the objective conditions of any cleavage require individual leadership and inspiration. This is even more true of subjective conditions. Differences of opinion remain politically inconsequential until mobilised. Nevertheless, finding objective support for the presence of a cleavage would go a long way toward providing evidence that the cleavage is there to influence voters. It is the search for evidence supporting the presence of the core–periphery cleavage that will occupy many of the pages below.

## Patterns of class voting in British politics

Class has been the dominant influence on British politics since at least 1945. During the heyday of this alignment, British society was divided into two groups: a homogeneous unionised working class and a somewhat more hetero-geneous middle class. Paralleling the class conflict within society, two large, class-based party groupings dominated the political spectrum and regularly captured over 90 per cent of the vote and all but a handful of the seats in Parliament. Labour and the Conservatives defined themselves on the basis of class issues: extensions to the welfare state, nationalisation, alternative taxation strategies, and public versus private provision of education, infrastructure, and housing services. It appeared that Labour's appeal was limited almost exclusively to the working class while the Conservatives had more cross-class support.

British politics have not always been locked into a class mould. The great Liberal–Conservative struggles of the nineteenth century were not predicated on the division of society into conflicting, hierarchically organised classes. Class conflict is a conflict between high status and low status groups that are defined in terms of their relationship to the means of production. The Victorian parties defined themselves primarily in terms of sectarian, mode of production (landed versus industrialist interests), and imperialist issues. Class, as defined by the owner-versus-worker cleavage, emerged as the defining element of the parties, and thereby of British politics, only after Labour replaced the Liberal Party in the aftermath of the First World War.[26]

Nor did the British political debate seem likely to remain fixed in a class-based mode. The first surveys of British voting behaviour noted that the hold of class seemed to be weaker among the young than the old. More recent work suggests that voters are not strongly attached to any party and that they vote according to the immediate issues of an election.[27] Some argue that the defining parameters of British politics are in a state of slow flux: from a religious basis to a class basis, and now to a post-industrial 'new politics' basis, where the debate is over quality of life issues rather than quantity and distribution of economic benefits.[28] Yet aggregate and survey data suggest that the move to 'new politics' is not occurring and that class remains paramount.[29]

Although these studies have done much to challenge the unfreezing or dealignment argument, neither the aggregate-level nor the survey-based approach has been able to explain the increasing divergence of party support between north and south. Despite the intellectual energy expended in exploring the north–south divide, the phenomenon remains a paradox. Dealignment, socio-economic change, migration, changes in aggregate or individual economic conditions, and variations in individual perceptions of changes in their economic conditions have all been examined, and found wanting as explanations for the situation.[30]

This book investigates the north–south divide from a perspective that accepts the hypothesis that the class cleavage has been loosened, or, in the Rokkanian sense, has become 'unfrozen'. Far from transforming British politics, however, the unfreezing has allowed cleavages that had been buried or overwhelmed, specifically the core–periphery cleavage, to re-emerge to influence the pattern of electoral support in ways similar to support before the First World War. By focusing on long-term change, this investigation offers an explanation for electoral change that goes beyond the bumps and scrapes of everyday political economy. Starting from the premise that the freezing hypothesis is essentially correct, this study examines contemporary electoral developments within the historical and geographical context of the British polity.

## THE STARTING POINT: 1885

The middle of the nineteenth century was a period of frequent and significant reform. Beginning with the first Reform Acts of 1832, and continuing in fits and starts through what have become known as the third Reform Acts of 1884, Britain underwent great changes in the way it handled relations between people and the state. Dissenters and Roman Catholics gained political and social rights; members of the working classes began to be enfranchised; representation became more equitable with the reduction in rotten boroughs – urban seats with so few voters that an individual or group of individuals could buy their votes – and redistribution of parliamentary constituency boundaries; and agriculture became exposed to foreign competition. Through much of the period these changes had little impact on the elected élites because Britain was in the midst of a long period of prosperity, of rising wages without commensurate inflationary pressures, and of good employment opportunities for all but the least skilled workers. The Victorian élite of landlords, industrialists and church leaders, and the majority of their electors, rolled in unprecedented wealth.

The prosperity came to an end in 1880. Imported agricultural products depressed landlord incomes and stopped the good times in the country. Increased industrialisation in other countries boosted competition for English industry and put a similar halt to the good times in the industrial areas. Disenchantment among the voters affected the elected officials.

Three more changes mark the 1880s as a break in the continuity of British politics. First, the independent MP, documented by Lowell's counting of roll-call votes, was in terminal decline; divisions whipped by the government climbed from 49 per cent of all divisions in 1836 to around 90 per cent in 1881, and stayed there through the rest of the century.[31] Connected with this was the development of the mass party as a group of committed members led by professional politicians, itself a partial offshoot of the Ballot Act of 1872 which created the secret ballot and thereby destroyed the power of rural landlords.[32] Finally, political unrest in Ireland moved from a small but distracting issue for the elected élite to a burning and divisive issue for the electorate as a whole. Hanham suggests that

> [t]he break in English political life, in so far as there was one, came not in 1867 but in the years between 1880 and 1886.
>
> The general election of 1874 was the last to take place in the old conditions. By 1880 the Home Rule movement had grown from small and very respectable beginnings to become a real menace to the English supremacy in Ireland. The Home Rulers had also put an end to many of the comforts which had made parliamentary life so agreeable to English country gentlemen ... Much of the remaining flavour of mid-Victorian politics also disappeared with the death of Disraeli in 1881 ... and was never recaptured. The Conservative party which he had done so much to create took on a new rôle [*sic*] only

five years after his death, when the Liberal party finally collapsed as a result of its many internal conflicts.[33]

The year 1885 also marks the first election where more than half the adult male population had the vote.[34] With new party leaders leading more cohesive parties, new élite relations with a greatly expanded electorate, and the growing importance of a different set of religious issues, 1885 marked a new era and the dawn of modern British politics. It is appropriate to begin the quantitative part of this study with this year.

METHODOLOGY

Examinations of historical dimensions of social, economic, and political trends are faced with the problem of selecting the investigative method most suitable to the period under discussion and the resources at hand. Much history, including social history, takes the form of biography: reading accounts of individual actions and reflections to gain, for example, a sense of social structure. When the focus is a historical event rather than an individual, history takes the form of qualitative research.[35] The overall effect is a visual panorama of events. For some periods, especially the more recent ones, this sort of analysis can be supplemented with discussions of social reality based on attitudinal data or quantitative research. Carefully constructed surveys targeting members of a certain social group, voting cohort, or city can provide illuminating information on why people do the things they do. Again, the result can be a vivid painting of life at a certain point in time, of the forces involved in a social movement, or of the processes by which individuals come to certain decisions. Added to the visual image, though, are answers to questions of 'how much' and 'how many'.

A less visual source of information comes from aggregate-level data collected contemporaneously with the event under discussion: census data can tell observers how many people were doing what sorts of things and living in which types of situation. Data on election results, head of cattle, prices and quantities of goods sold, or population density and per capita income give quantified indicators of the visual imagery portrayed through biographical research.

There is a place in historical political analysis for all these approaches. The selection of one data method over another depends on the availability of the various types of data, the research topic under discussion, and the personal preferences of the observer. Not all methods are equally suitable for any specific project, even if the data exist at all levels. A judicious evaluation of the research topic and the availability of resources provides grounds for the proper selection of research techniques.

While survey evidence would be a very useful tool for measuring the spatial dimension of individual attitudes toward core and periphery, the earliest surveys in our arsenal date from the 1940s; such a limited time period is completely inadequate for relating the social patterns of the 1980s and 1990s to the late nineteenth century. Furthermore, the question of individual feelings about the appropriate level of centralisation of the British government was not asked before 1970. The available data limit our examination to the level of aggregate voting behaviour and group characteristics on the one hand, and to the study of biographical materials on the other.

Biographies and explorations of historical documents are a second avenue of research that can yield information about the distribution of attitudes towards the central government and related matters. Content analysis of newspapers, covering an extended period of years, can reveal the extent to which information about one part of the country is transmitted to other parts. Such an exploration could uncover the broad contours of core and periphery throughout Britain at different points in time. There would be a difficulty, however, in defining the contours more explicitly: the relative importance of the major cities could probably be gauged, but the counties between are likely to remain something of a black hole.[36] The same problem exists for other types of qualitative approach: while suggestive, qualitative investigation is not likely to cover Britain with enough detail for the project discussed here.

The most readily available source of information distinguishing regions of Britain is aggregate-level data. Due to the near-constancy of county boundaries between 1885 and 1972, and the preference of the British government for publishing data at no lower a level before about 1918, the county is the unit of analysis for this investigation. Most of the available census data have already been examined for evidence of one sort of electoral influence or another. This study will build on these earlier analyses, adding other data where relevant, to evaluate the importance of the core–periphery cleavage since 1885.

The main elements of the argument revolve around the development of a *dynamic* model where core and periphery are defined according to economic and socio-cultural conditions. The construction identifies variables that are indicators of core and periphery status and that are available throughout the entire century since 1885. Values for these variables are gathered for 1891, 1921, 1951 and 1991 for all counties in England, Scotland and Wales and combined into a total of four core–periphery variables, one for each collection period. These are then used to examine the changing dimensions of core and periphery and to track the continuing relationship between the core–periphery matrix and voting.

### NOTES

1.  C. Pattie, E. Fieldhouse, R. Johnston, and A. Russell, 'A Widening Regional Cleavage in British Voting Behaviour: Some Preliminary Explanations', in I. Crewe, P. Norris, D. Denver, and D. Broughton (eds), *British Elections and Parties Yearbook: 1991* (London: Harvester Wheatsheaf, 1992) pp. 130–41.
2.  Speech in London, quoted in R. Martin, 'The Political Economy of Britain's North–South Divide', in J. Lewis and A. Townsend (eds), *The North–South Divide: Regional Change in Britain in the 1980s* (London: Paul Chapman, 1989) p. 21. The completely erroneous assumptions about wealth creation that lie behind this assertion are astonishing. Rubenstein makes it clear that the south has been the centre of wealth creation since at least 1800. See W. D. Rubenstein, 'British Millionaires, 1809–1949', *Bulletin of the Institute of Historical Research*, 47, 116 (November 1974) pp. 202–23; W. D. Rubenstein, 'Wealth, Elites, and the Class Structure of Modern Britain', *Past and Present*, 76 (August 1977) pp. 99–126; and W. D. Rubenstein, 'Victorian Middle Classes: Wealth, Occupation, and Geography', *Economic History Review*, 30, 4 (December 1977) pp. 602–23.
3.  D. Butler and D. Kavanagh, *The British General Election of 1992* (London:

Macmillan, 1992), p. 247; A. Heath, R. Jowell, and J. Curtice, 'Can Labour Win?' in A. Heath, R. Jowell, and J. Curtice, with B. Taylor (eds), *Labour's Last Chance? The 1992 Election and Beyond* (Aldershot: Dartmouth, 1994), pp. 281–4.

4. C. Pattie, *et al.*, pp. 140–1.; I. McAllister and D. T. Studlar, 'Region and Voting in Britain 1979-87: Territorial Polarization or Artifact?', *American Journal of Political Science*, 36, 1 (February 1992), pp. 168–99.

5. Examples of this work include J. Curtice, 'One Nation?', in R. Jowell, S. Witherspoon, and L. Brook (eds), *British Social Attitudes: The Fifth Report* (Aldershot: Gower, 1988); A. F. Heath, R. Jowell, J. Curtice, G. Evans, J. Field, and S. Witherspoon, *Understanding Political Change: The British Voter, 1964–1987* (Oxford: Pergamon Press, 1991); J. Lewis and A. Townsend, *The North–South Divide: Regional Change in Britain in the 1980s* (London: Paul Chapman, 1989); I. McAllister and D. T. Studlar; D. McMahon, A. F. Heath, M. Harrop, and J. Curtice, 'The Electoral Consequences of North– South Migration', *British Journal of Political Science*, 22, 4 (October 1992), pp. 419-44; K. Jones, R. J. Johnston, and C. J. Pattie, 'People, Places, and Regions: Exploring the Use of Multi-Level Modeling in the Analysis of Electoral Data', *British Journal of Political Science*, 22, 3 (July 1992), pp. 343–80; R. J. Johnston, C. J. Pattie, and J. G. Allsop, *A Nation Dividing? The Electoral Map of Great Britain, 1979–87* (London: Longman, 1988).

6. K. Wald, *Crosses on the Ballot: Patterns of British Voter Alignment Since 1885* (Princeton: Princeton University Press, 1983); N. Blewett, *The Peers the Parties, and the People* (London: Macmillan, 1972). See Chapter 2 below, however.

7. J. A. Hobson, 'The General Election: A Sociological Interpretation', *The Sociological Review*, 32 (April 1910) pp. 105–17; V. Bogdanor and W. H. Field, 'Lessons of History: Core and Periphery in British Electoral Behaviour, 1910–1992', *Electoral Studies*, 12, 3 (Sept. 1993) pp. 204–24.

8. E. R. A. N. Smith, *The Unchanging American Voter* (Berkeley and Los Angeles: University of California Press, 1989) p. 1–2.

9. See R. J. Dalton, S. C. Flanagan, and P. A. Beck (eds), *Electoral Change in Advanced Industrial Democracies: Realignment or Dealignment* (Princeton: Princeton University Press, 1984); F. F. Piven (ed.), *Labour Parties in Post-industrial Societies* (Oxford: Polity Press, 1991); S. Holmberg, 'Party Identification Compared Across the Atlantic' in M. K. Jennings and T. E. Mann (eds), *Elections at Home and Abroad: Essays in Honor of Warren E. Miller* (Ann Arbor: University of Michigan Press, 1994) pp. 93–121. For a counter-argument, see S. Bartolini and P. Mair, *Identity, Competition and Electoral Availability: The Stabilisation of European Electorates 1885–1985* (Cambridge: Cambridge University Press, 1990); W. H. Field, 'Electoral Volatility and the Structure of Competition: A Reassessment of Voting Patterns in Britain 1959–92', *West European Politics*, 17, 4 (October 1994) pp. 149–65.

10. J. R. Owens, and L. L. Wade; K. Jones, R. J. Johnston, and C. Pattie; B. Paulson, 'The Economy and the 1992 Election: Was 1992 Labour's Golden Chance?' in A. Heath, R. Jowell, and J. Curtice, with B. Taylor (eds), *Labour's Last Chance? The 1992 Election and Beyond* (Aldershot: Dartmouth, 1994); D. Sanders and S. Price, 'Party Support and Economic Perceptions in the UK 1979–87: A Two-Level Approach', in D. Broughton, *et al.* (eds), *British Elections and Parties Yearbook 1994* (London: Frank Cass, 1995); D. Sanders, 'Economic Performance, Management Competence, and the Outcome of the Next General Election', *Political Studies*, 44, 2 (June 1996) pp. 203–31. See, however, H. D. Clarke and M. C. Stewart, 'Economic Evaluations and Electoral Outcomes: An Evaluation of Alternative Forecasting Models', in Broughton, *et al.* (eds), *British Elections and Parties Yearbook: 1994* (London: Frank Cass, 1995).

11. D. Butler and D. Stokes, *Political Change in Britain* (London: Macmillan 1969) p. 391.

12. I do not mean to suggest that party-system cleavages can have no effect on societal cleavages, nor that the government cannot influence societal and party-system cleavages in turn. The degree of influence that is possible, however, is directly related to the strength of societal cleavages: in systems in turmoil with weak cleavages, as in Russia today, parties and the government have substantially more influence than in systems with stable, entrenched societal cleavages.

13. S. M. Lipset and S. Rokkan, 'Cleavage Structures, Party Systems, and Voter Alignments: An Introduction', in S. M. Lipset and S. Rokkan (eds), *Party Systems and Voter Alignments* (New York: The Free Press, 1967) pp. 1–67.

14. Ibid., p. 52.

15. J. Ambler, 'Educational Pluralism in the French Fifth Republic', in J. F. Hollifield and G. Ross (eds), *Searching for the New France* (New York and London: Routledge, 1991) pp. 193–220.

16. Core and periphery are distinct from centre and periphery in so far as the 'centre' refers simply to the location of the central government. Rokkan and Urwin define the centre as 'privileged locations within a territory where key military, economic and cultural resource-holders most frequently meet', while their periphery is everything else. See S. Rokkan and D. Urwin, *The Politics of Territorial Identity: Studies in European Regionalism* (Beverly Hills, CA: Sage, 1982) p. 5. Centre–periphery relations in Britain concern the relationship between the central government at Westminster and all the local governments around Britain, including those in London. A core–periphery terminology defines the core as an area that includes the centre but which also has a long-maintained dominance over territory gained later. The areas that make up core and periphery in Britain will be explored and defined in the chapters below.

17. E. S. Wellhofer, 'Core and Periphery: Territorial Dimensions in Politics', *Urban Studies*, 26 (1989) p. 342.

18. S. M. Lipset and S. Rokkan, p. 50.

19. W. L. Miller, 'The De-Nationalisation of British Politics: The Re-Emergence of the Periphery', *West European Politics*, 6, 4 (October 1983) pp. 103–29.

20. M. Shamir, 'Are Western European Party Systems "Frozen"?', *Comparative Political Studies*, 17,1 (April 1984) pp. 35–79; and M. Maguire, 'Is There Still Persistence: Electoral Change in Western Europe, 1948–1979', in H. Daalder and P. Mair (eds), *Western European Party Systems: Continuity and Change* (London: Sage, 1979) both suggest increasing electoral instability in recent years. S. Bartolini and P. Mair suggest overall stability. Each of these studies looks at aggregate election results, noting the net change in overall party support from election to election.
    The following studies have examined regional change: R. J. Johnston, A. B. O'Neill, and P. J. Taylor, 'The Geography of Party Support: Comparative Studies in Electoral Stability', in M. J. Holler (ed.), *The Logic of Multiparty Systems* (Dordrecht: Kluwer Academic Publishers, 1987); J. Curtice and M. Steed, 'Electoral Choice and the Production of Government: The Changing Operation of the Electoral System in the United Kingdom Since 1955', *British Journal of Political Science*, 12, 3 (July 1982) pp. 249–98; and J. Curtice and M. Steed, 'Proportionality and Exaggeration in the British Electoral System', *Electoral Studies* 5, 3 (December 1986) pp. 209-28. The first of these begins with the first post-war elections and says nothing about the relation of the post-war period to the period when the franchise was first fully extended. The

latter two begin even later.

21. H. F. L. Cocks, *The Nonconformist Conscience* (London: Independent Press, 1943) p. 35.
22. The Macaulay quotation may be found in D. Urwin, 'Toward the Nationalization of British Politics?' in Otto Büsch (ed.), *Wählerbewegungen in der Europäischen Geschichte* (Berlin: Colloquium Verlag, 1980) p. 227. Gladstone's characterisation comes from W. E. Gladstone, 'The County Franchise and Mr. Lowe Thereon', *Nineteenth Century*, 2 (November 1877) p. 552. The Anglican Church was and is the Established Church of England, of which the monarch is the head. All church appointments are controlled by the government through the monarchy. Nonconformist churches are the various protestant groups that stand in opposition to the Established Church, chief among them are the Baptist and Methodist Churches. Nonconformists are also called Dissenters. Members of the Established Church referred to their house of worship as a church, while Dissenters referred to their houses as chapels, so a shorthand way of distinguishing the groups is to define them in terms of 'church 'and 'chapel'.
23. Quoted in Charles Stuart Parker (ed.), *Sir Robert Peel. From his Private Papers* (London: John Murray, 1891–99), Vol. 3, p. 8.
24. C. Matthew, R. McKibbin and J. Kay, 'The Franchise Factor in the Rise of the Labour Party', *English Historical Review*, 91, 361 (October 1976) pp. 723–52.
25. One usually places the Liberal party's persistent and seemingly inexplicable strength during the interwar period in such agricultural areas as East Anglia in this category. Liberal survival elsewhere in the 1950s has often been attributed to the residual effects of prior electoral attachments.
26. N. Blewett; K. D. Wald. See E. S. Wellhofer, *Democracy, Capitalism and Empire in Late Victorian Britain* (London: Macmillan, 1996) for an alternative analysis.
27. D. Butler and D. Stokes; H. T. Himmelweit, P. Humphreys, and M. Jaeger, *How Voters Decide*, revised ed. (Milton Keynes: Open University, 1985); R. Rose and I. MacAllister, *Voters Begin to Choose: From Closed Class to Open Elections in Britain* (London: Sage, 1986).
28. R. Inglehart, *Culture Shift in Advanced Industrial Society* (Princeton: Princeton University Press, 1990).
29. A. F. Heath, *et al.* (1994); Bartolini and Mair; W. H. Field.
30. On dealignment, see R. J. Johnston and C. J. Pattie, 'Class Dealignment and the Regional Polarization of Voting Patterns in Great Britain 1964–1987', *Political Geography Quarterly*, 11, 1 (January 1992), pp. 73–86. On migration, see D. McMahon, A. F. Heath, M. Harrop and J. Curtice. On economic conditions, see J. R. Owens and L. L. Wade; I. McAllister and D. Studlar; and R. J. Johnston, C. J. Pattie and J. G. Allsop. These studies will be examined more fully in Chapter 3 below.
31. G. W. Cox, *The Efficient Secret: The Cabinet and the Development of Political Parties in Victorian England* (Cambridge: Cambridge University Press, 1987) p. 24. Derived from calculations by A. Lawrence Lowell, *The Government of England*, 2nd ed. (New York: Macmillan, 1919).
32. M. Ostrogorski, *Democracy and the Organisation of Political Parties*, reprinted 1970 (London: Haskell House, 1902), Vol. II, p. 370.
33. H. J. Hanham, *Elections and Party Management: Politics in the Time of Disraeli and Gladstone* (London: Longman, 1959) p. xvi.
34. C. Matthew, R. McKibbin, and J. Kay.
35. For a work in which this is the focus, see F. M. L. Thompson, *The Cambridge Social History of Britain 1750–1950* (Cambridge: Cambridge University Press, 1990).

36. The scene from the BBC Television satire *Yes, Prime Minister* that deals with the possibility of moving military bases illustrates this problem quite well. As portrayed in the sixth episode, the military establishment does not want to move to the north of England nor Scotland because of the distance from Harrods and Wimbledon that such a relocation would create.

# CHAPTER TWO

# The Electoral Geography of Britain, 1885-1992

TWO THINGS are necessary in order to appreciate how contemporary regional differences that result from core and periphery have affected electoral dynamics in Britain: first, an understanding of core and periphery, and second, a grasp of regional electoral change. This second requirement has embedded in it more than simply a quantitative display of regional votes; a more qualitative understanding of political issues and élite perceptions is also needed. Electoral change goes beyond election results. The primary aim of this chapter is to trace, briefly, the modern electoral history of Britain with a special emphasis on its regional dimension. The evidence shows the extent to which British political parties have attracted balanced national support or, conversely, whether their electoral base has been restricted to specific regions of the country.

The terms 'north' and 'south' will have relevance throughout this volume. Unless otherwise noted, the 'south' refers to London, the Home Counties, East Anglia, the counties of Cornwall, Devon, Dorset, Somerset, Hampshire, Wiltshire, Gloucestershire, Lincolnshire, and the Midlands. The 'north' includes Scotland, Wales, the ancient counties of Lancashire and Yorkshire, and the hill country up to the Scottish border. In later chapters where the distinction between north and south may be drawn differently, any changes will be carefully described.

This chapter places the chapters that follow into their proper historical context. As we shall see, voting outcomes result from a complex mixture of personal decisions amid structural parameters that shape individual choices and aggregate results. Some of these parameters are institutional, including the breadth of the franchise, the mechanism for translating votes into seats, and the rigidities of societal cleavages that develop into partisan loyalties. Changes in the franchise are likely to affect voting outcomes if the expansion brings a new social group with unevenly distributed partisan choices into the electoral arena. War, changes in party leadership, and social transformation are also likely to have an impact on the spatial distribution of party support. These many influences are not the focus of this analysis but knowledge of the social, political, and economic context of the voting decision is especially important when judging the cause of that decision. We shall begin with a brief discussion of events to 1885 and bring the reader chronologically up to the present period.

## ELECTORAL DEVELOPMENTS TO 1885

The Franchise Act of 1884 expanded the British electorate from about 35 per cent of all men aged 21 and above, to about 60 per cent of these men.[1] While the exclusion of women continued, it was possible for the first time to suggest that Britain was making substantial progress toward the principle of universal male suffrage. Four factors set the framework for the development of the modern mass parties today: the Corrupt Practices Act of 1883, the Redistribution Act of 1885, the Registration Act of 1885, and the near doubling of the electorate in 1884.[2] The year 1885 marks an evolutionary leap in the development of British democracy.

The late nineteenth century differed greatly from preceding years in a socio-economic sense as well as an electoral one. Mid-nineteenth century Britain was an aristocratic country. The upper echelons of the social structure ruled all below them, not by written privileges but by general acceptance and what Walter Bagehot called a deference to one's social betters. In 1867 the Radical writer Leslie Stephen explained matters in the following manner:

> The main influence ... of the upper classes undoubtedly depends upon what may be called the occult and unacknowledged forces which are not dependent upon any legislative machinery. England is still an aristocratic country ... because the whole upper and middle, and a great part of the lower, classes have still an instinctive liking for the established order of things; because innumerable social ties bind us together spontaneously, so as to give to the aristocracy a position tolerably corresponding to their political privileges.[3]

This was not true by 1910; large-scale industrialisation had transformed vast swathes of northern England, Wales, and Scotland into hotbeds of lower-class Radicalism that rejected the privileges of the aristocracy. In the 1860s, however, despite the democratic demands of the generally unenfranchised Chartists, the aristocracy was still pivotal across all significant political groupings.

Before 1885 the composition of the House of Commons had little to do with the 'will of the people'. The situation had been even worse before the 1867 Reform Acts, as an 1841 complaint by the Liberal Party's chief election agent, Joseph Parkes, suggests:

> [T]he action of *political* principle and particular Cabinet policies on the English Borough Constituencies is much overrated; ... the returns are much more influenced by particular *local* circumstances and the particular personal relations of *Candidates* than is generally imagined; ... the returns are greatly influenced by the *sufficiency* and *purse weight* of Candidates; [and] ... the Borough results in England generally much baffle previous calculations of both parties.[4]

The problem of rotten boroughs was substantially resolved in 1867, although about 30 seats, such as Sutherland and Argyllshire in the Scottish Highlands, remained under the control of a single landlord until at least 1885.[5] The electorate nearly doubled, but only to about 20 per cent of the adult male population, or about two million people.[6] The distribution of votes between constituencies remained far from even, and many Members of Parliament continued to be returned unopposed.[7] G. J. Holyoake complained to an audience of working men in 1868 that

> [t]hough Representation is open to us, we cannot understand too soon, that the House of Commons, like the London Tavern – is only open to those who can pay the tariff ... All that the sons of labour have gained at present, is the advantage of being consulted. Whoever is member will have to take them into account. This is a great thing gained. But the electoral machinery is centuries old; and the people cannot expect to come into possession of it without conditions, nor to master its use all at once.[8]

Translating the 'will of the people' into national government policy was becoming somewhat easier but it still involved a number of barriers, including an unrepresentative electorate, parochial local politics, unlimited campaign expenditure allowances, rotten seats where voting outcomes differed from projections, and MPs who were formally or *de facto* independent of any party whip. One of David Lloyd George's earliest political memories concerned the election of 1868, when farmers were evicted from their land because, in defiance of the landlord, they had voted in support of the victorious Liberal challenger to the Conservative incumbent in Caernarfon. In a speech to the newly enfranchised voters of Merthyr Tydfil at the same election, the radical Non-conformist Henry Richard phrased the complaints of the Welsh farmers against their English landlords in the following way:

> The people who speak this language [i.e., Welsh], who read this literature, who own this history, who inherit these traditions, who venerate these names, who created and sustain these marvellous religious organisations, the people forming three fourths of the people of Wales – have they not a right to say to this small propertied class ... We are the Welsh people and not you? This is our

country and not yours, and therefore we claim to have our principles and sentiments and feelings represented in the Commons' House of Parliament.[9]

As these circumstances were confounded with the problem of uncontested seats, drawing conclusions between the overall social geography of the country and electoral results is exceedingly, and probably hopelessly, difficult.

While the Liberals won and held a majority of the Scottish seats as early as 1832, the party did not capture Wales until 1865. Thus, the regional aspect of British politics that characterised late Victorian electoral geography had not yet fully evolved. Nevertheless, in order to trace the regional aspects of electoral returns it is useful to sketch the élite structure and social bases of the main parties. The Liberals dominated the House of Commons between 1832 and 1867. Their slender majority of English and Welsh seats (2,300 contested seats to 1,985 seats won by the Conservatives) was augmented by the consistent capture of 60 per cent and more of the Scottish and Irish seats; as a result, the party won seven of the period's nine general elections. The importance of the periphery to the Liberal Party is already evident in the party's reliance on these to enable it to form the government.

Following the enlargement of the electorate and a redistribution of seats in 1867, and contrary to expectations, the Liberals and Conservatives were evenly matched. Several students of the period have argued that the second Reform Act (1867) ushered in modern parties by replacing the politics of influence with the politics of electoral pressure, destroying the Burkean notion of the independent MP, and preparing the way for class politics along the cleavage lines defined by Marx.[10] Yet, although Gladstone could say in 1863 that 'Every person, not presumably incapacitated by some consideration of personal unfitness or political danger, is morally entitled to come within the pale of the Constitution', not until 1885 did even half of the adult male population gain the suffrage. Gladstone could write in 1868 that the 'movement of the public mind has been of a nature entirely transcending former experience; and ... it has likewise been more promptly and more effectively represented, than at any earlier period, in the action of the Government and the Legislature'.[11] Nevertheless, the 'public' was still a middle-class and aristocratically deferential organism and not a collectivist class of workers. Thus, while events and allegiances laid in the years leading up to 1885 had their impact in the following years, that year marks a social and political turning point for the British political system.

## Party developments

The year 1885 marks a turning point to the party system too. Religious differences first found explicit partisan expression during the middle years of the nineteenth century. The rise of the new Liberal Party in the 1830s gave parliamentary structure to the Anglican–Nonconformist differences that had simmered since the English Civil War. Nonconformists flocked to the new party, and it quickly formed the government. Among the first laws passed by the new party was the Marriage Act and Tithe Commutation Act of 1836 which cemented the allegiance of Nonconformists through official and legal recognition of non-Anglican weddings, and the exemption of Dissenters from the obligation of tithing to the Established Church.

The fundamental support for the Conservatives lay in the landowning classes who were overwhelmingly Anglican and English.[12] This gave the party both a religious and a regional base that survived its near-total disruption following Peel's repeal of the Corn Laws in 1846. Between 1846 and 1885, the Conservative Party's defence of the Union with Ireland solidified its strength in the Established Church and alienated members of Nonconformist churches.

Between 1846 and 1885, a heterogeneous alliance of Peelite, Whig, Liberal and Radical élites dominated a large segment of the British political spectrum and the House of Commons.[13] The loose grouping eventually coalesced into the Gladstonian Liberal Party, but, given the initial diversity of the alliance, its religious base was still rather tenuous in these years. Early support for the Nonconformist cause brought a sizeable number of Dissenters into the group as Liberals, but they did not always fit well with the urban interests of

Anglican industrialists and non-Radical party supporters. Gladstone's support for Irish Home Rule in 1885, however, drove Joseph Chamberlain to lead Anglicans, who opposed Home Rule, to cross the floor to sit as Liberal Unionists. While reducing the pool of potential Liberal supporters, the departure of the Liberal Unionists created a certain religious purity in the party and allowed it to espouse the views of the periphery more clearly. Over the ensuing elections many Anglican Liberals stayed with the Liberal Unionists and eventually joined the Conservative and Unionist Party. Between 1886 and 1910, Liberal electoral support came primarily from Nonconformists and lower-class but enfranchised radicals in industrial areas.

The religious bases of Liberal and Conservative Party support were thus consolidated during the period leading up to, and immediately following, the reforms of 1883–85. Liberal support became strongest in areas of the greatest Nonconformist feeling: Wales, Scotland, Cornwall, Lancashire, and northern England. Ireland became a bastion of the Irish Nationalists, who also managed to hold one seat in Liverpool between 1885 and 1910.[14] Electoral politics in the United Kingdom thus exhibited a strong regional dimension by the end of the century. The high congruence between Nonconformity and regions of high Liberal support suggests that religion was the primary defining characteristic of the electoral stage during the late Victorian and Edwardian periods.[15]

## Political issues

The salient political issues of the time grew from the religious cleavage, with the most intransigent ones revolving around Irish (Catholic) Home Rule, the disestablishment of the Welsh Church, and discrimination against those who refused to adopt the rituals of the Anglican Church. These controversies directly concerned the power of the central government *vis-à-vis* power centres that were more distant from London, and as such can clearly be labelled as core–periphery issues. Additional non-religious issues included tariff and tax policies, women's suffrage, and the role of the House of Lords in making or blocking legislation. With the exception of the extension of the suffrage to women, these issues were also of a core–periphery nature, revolving as they did around localised versus centralised control over social, economic, and cultural conditions and institutions. The Irish Home Rule question was an issue of British imperialism. Calls for Disestablishment, the end of religious discrimination, and a reduction in the power of the Lords were all attempts to increase local control at the expense of the centralised state.

The freezing hypothesis put forth by Stein Rokkan suggests that this cleavage, whether it was religious or regional (or both) in its essence, should have remained influential on the British political stage even after the resolution of the issues that shaped this cleavage. This did not happen. Miller and Wald both argue that the resolution of most of these issues in the years before the First World War, coupled with the expansion of the franchise in 1918, put an end to religion as the dominant cleavage while introducing a class cleavage instead.[16] Regional differences faded for several decades, only to re-emerge with a vengeance from about 1955 to the present. Interpreting these regional differences as a result of core–periphery conflict explains a lot of the variation, as the following sections will show.

## THE GEOGRAPHY OF ELECTIONS, 1885–1910

The general election of 1886 heralded 20 years of hegemony by the allied Conservative and Liberal Unionist Parties. This alliance, henceforth called the Unionists, won an absolute majority of seats and votes in Britain in all four elections of the period up to 1900. The 1892 election saw a decline in Conservative support in Protestant Ireland, which cost them their overall majority in Westminster, but it was not until 1906 that the Liberals were truly able to mount an effective opposition to the Unionist strength in Britain. By 1910 a Unionist resurgence forced the Liberal government to depend on support from the Irish Nationalist Party and the new Labour Party for the maintenance of its majority.

An early outburst of Welsh nationalism erupted in 1895,

when David Lloyd George adopted a programme advocating self-government for Wales through a new organisation, *Cymru Fydd*. As with the electoral successes of Plaid Cymru since the late 1960s, Lloyd George gathered considerable support for his cause from rural regions, but failed to secure the support of the more urban and Anglicised south Wales. The struggle over political control of local power centres was already lost in industrial Wales, since English landlords were viewed less as alien oppressors when much of the population was itself English. Concerning the failure of *Cymru Fydd*, Lloyd George wrote to his wife that 'Welsh Wales is with us';[17] the problem for Welsh nationalism, then, as now, was that Wales is English as well as Welsh.

For its part, Scottish nationalism, or at least Home Rule, was a major plank of the Gladstonian Liberal Party. The Scottish Liberal Association voted for Home Rule in 1888, and, with the Irish Home Rule movement gaining strength in Ireland and in Britain, many Scots felt that a Scottish Parliament would be created soon after the Liberals formed a government with a safe majority. From then until 1914 a steady stream of doomed Home Rule Bills was presented to Parliament. Eventually the Liberal Prime Minister Herbert Asquith, envisaging a Scottish Parliament as part of a wider reform in the United Kingdom, pushed a Home Rule Bill through two readings in 1914 before the war intervened and political reforms were shelved.[18]

A more radical and more explicitly Scottish Home Rule movement evolved out of land wars between landless peasants (crofters) and their landlords, and led to the creation in the 1880s of the Highland Land League and the Crofters' Party. The agitation of these groups was predicated on two connected ideas: first, that certain wrongs had been committed against the Highlanders by the English and, second, that these wrongs could be righted if the Scottish were to rule themselves. The considerable Home Rule activism that these parties pursued found its way into the Liberal Party platform through an electoral pact that the Crofters' Party forged with the Liberals. The source of the two strands of the Home Rule activism of the 1970s to the 1990s can be found in this period: the general devolution movement of the modern-day Liberal Democrats (and, to a lesser extent, Labour) comes from Gladstone and Asquith, while the more anti-English rhetoric is alive and well in the Scottish National Party.

This period, and especially the 1906 and the 1910 elections, were dominated by a handful of issues, most of which were of a decidedly core–periphery nature: Irish Home Rule, Welsh Disestablishment, the equity of government funding for Anglican church schools but not Dissenting schools, and the power of the House of Lords. As these issues worked their way through the electorate and the parties, the battle lines between core and periphery, between Crown and country, became more and more pronounced. In 1910, *Blackwood's Magazine* reported that political fervour for the Liberal Party closely followed religious fervour for the Nonconformist sects: 'Every Pleasant [*sic*] Sunday Afternoon sent forth a horde of canvassers, convinced by much turgid oratory that the cause of Liberalism was the cause of God.'[19] Showing its own political colours, the *Standard* complained that same year about the 'ferocious partisan harangues … delivered on the Sabbath to a congregation supposed to be assembled for religious worship'.[20] The active intervention of religious leaders in the political arena is apparent.

Figure 2.1 shows the widening gap in Conservative support in the south of England compared with the rest of Britain. Whereas Unionist support was broadly similar in north and south in 1885, before the Liberal split, this became increasingly less true as time went on. The only exception is 1906, where, in a landslide, the Liberals and their Labour allies were able to win a large number of the seats in the south as well as slightly more than their usual share in the north. In other elections, the Unionists won 60 to 80 per cent of the southern seats, while Labour and the Liberals won between one-half and two-thirds of the seats in the north up to 1900 and over three-quarters of them in 1910.

The increasing regional divergence in electoral support is to be noted here. The split in the Liberal Party before the election of 1886 opened the regional divide which held steady through the period of strongest Unionist strength and then widened as the Liberals regained support in the later

FIGURE 2.1
CONSERVATIVE STRENGTH IN NORTH AND SOUTH,
1885–DECEMBER 1910

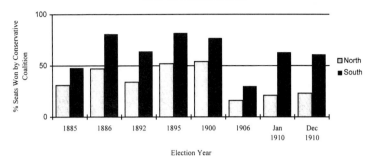

Northern seats are those in, and north of, the counties of Yorkshire and Lancashire in England, and all Scottish and Welsh seats. The Irish Nationalist seat is counted in the Liberal and Labour grouping.
Source: N. Blewett, *The Peers, the Parties, and the People* (London: Macmillan, 1973) p. 383.

elections. In 1910 the Liberal sociologist J. A. Hobson was moved to declare:

> The two Englands to which the electoral map gives substantially accurate expression, may be described as a Producer's England and a Consumer's England, one England in which the well-to-do classes, from their numbers, wealth, leisure and influence, mould the external character of the civilisation and determine the habits, feelings and opinions of the people, the other England in which the structure and activities of large organised industries, carried on by great associated masses of artisans, factory hands and miners are the dominating facts and forces.[21]

Social and economic change had altered patron–client and class relations in the north, but Leslie Stephen's comments of 1867 still held sway in the south.[22] This socio-economic expression of the core–periphery cleavage is evident in these remarks; we shall return to them later.

ELECTORAL DEVELOPMENTS IN THE INTER-WAR PERIOD

British politics underwent considerable turmoil during the inter-war period. A general election occurred on average every three years, compared with an average time of nearly four years between elections in the pre-war and post-war periods. Party fortunes fluctuated dramatically, with the Conservatives generally in the ascendancy but with Labour leading a government for the first time. With the departure of Ireland and the satisfaction of many of the demands made by the Dissenters, the economic and social expression of the core–periphery cleavage became more muted during this period and its electoral expression also declined.

## The collapse of the Liberal Party

The Great War coincided with a shattering of the Liberal Party, although the actual reasons for the fragmentation are still in dispute. There are three main avenues of explanation, each of which has merit. Some are more supportive of the core–periphery explanation of British politics than others. Let us review the relative strength of each of these explanations in turn.

### Élite dissent and ideological confusion

The first explanation finds the cause in *élite dissent*. A somewhat reluctant Herbert Asquith led an even more reluctant party into the First World War. As the crisis with Germany threatened to erupt into war, many in the party agreed with H. N. Brailsford's condemnation of its causes as a 'war of steel and gold'.[23] Nevertheless, once the war began public opinion quickly condemned, not the crisis, but Germany's role in it. Edward Grey explained the new Liberal position to the House of Commons:

> If, in a crisis like this, we run away from those obligations of honour and interest as regards the Belgian Treaty, I doubt whether, whatever material force we might have at the end, it would be of very much value in the face of the respect we should have lost.[24]

Although Liberal opinion generally swung behind the decision to honour treaty obligations and enter the war, some members of the government expressed considerable reservations about it and Charles Trevelyan even resigned from the government in protest. The end of the war found this prominent Liberal a member of the Labour Party, and later an advocate of a Popular Front with the Communists.[25]

At the outset of the war the Liberals abandoned their electoral machinery and devoted themselves completely to harnessing Britain's industrial might to the war effort. All parties declared an electoral truce, but Labour and the Conservatives continued to nurture their ties with the electorate. By 1915, the government became increasingly debilitated over internal dissension over the proper balance to strike between the overwhelming needs of victory and the maintenance of Liberal ideals. Despite the calling of an electoral truce at the beginning of the war, Conservative attacks on the Liberals' perceived mismanagement of the war effort, coupled with the government's own difficulty with its backbenchers, convinced the Chancellor of the Exchequer David Lloyd George and the Conservative leader Andrew Bonar Law that a coalition was necessary. With Asquith's acquiescence but without discussion with other party notables, the last Liberal government ended in May 1915.

The Liberal Party split in 1916 over the twin issues of whether to introduce conscription and who to support as party leader. These were interrelated insofar as 'the people who wanted compulsory service did not want Asquith, whilst the supporters of Asquith did not want conscription.'[26] When Asquith resigned from the government in 1916, Lloyd George became Prime Minister, but only one other Liberal agreed to serve in the coalition War Cabinet, and the backbenchers were divided. Many were hostile toward the government but, as Asquith refused officially to oppose the government until May 1918, their hostility was generally without direction. Quoting an unnamed Conservative politician, John Maynard Keynes called them 'a lot of hard-faced men ... who look as if they had done very well out of the war'.[27] Asquith, by contrast, kept the Liberal conscience.

Asquith and Lloyd George entered the 1918 and 1922

elections at the head of two separate parties. Thinking that the Liberals could stand alone against Labour and the Conservatives, Asquith led an independent Liberal Party into the elections. Lloyd George and the Conservative leader Bonar Law both thought that continued Liberal–Conservative co-operation was necessary as an antidote to the socialist overtones of the rising Labour Party. With the passing of many of the core–periphery issues that had divided Liberals from Conservatives, Bonar Law confessed to a political friend that 'I do not think anyone can doubt … that our party on the old lines will never have any future again in this country'.[28]

Lloyd George led 157 'couponed' Liberals into the 1918 election.[29] A disproportionate number of his 133 successful candidates were in Wales and Scotland, while 38 of the 90 English victories were in the periphery, including 27 in Yorkshire and Lancashire. The Asquith Liberals wanted a stand-alone party, but the 28 elected members out of 253 candidates were too scattered to make a viable opposition. Lloyd George's group, renamed the National Liberals following the dissolution of the coalition, were similarly devastated in 1922, returning only 62 members out of 162 candidates (35 of which were in the periphery), as Labour emerged as the second largest party. Liberal candidates without allegiance to either leader won a handful of seats in rural Scotland and Wales, and a scattering of seats in the English periphery. The leadership struggles after 1916 devastated the Liberal Party.

When the Conservative Party again took up the cause of protectionism just before the 1923 general election, the various Liberal factions patched over their differences to present a reunited party, but the party could not maintain its internal cohesion for long. A three-way split occurred in 1931 that resulted in one group, the National Liberals (also called the Simonite Liberals) eventually joining the Conservatives with the others reuniting once again after the 1935 election. Dissension between Liberal leaders over policies and personalities again fractured party solidarity. Voter loyalty to long-sitting Liberal MPs in the Scottish Highlands was about all that kept the party from losing its electoral base completely. Differences in policy, leadership struggles, and confusion about whether socialism or capitalism was the greater evil all contributed to these internal disputes. Naturally, the disputes did not help the party's electoral fortunes.

*Franchise changes*

A second possible reason for the reduction of the Liberals to minor party status was the *expansion of the franchise*: in 1918 the vote was extended to include 95 per cent of men over 21 (up from 60 per cent since 1885), and most women over 29. All property and income requirements were abolished. The middle-class share of the electorate fell from 40 per cent to 20 per cent as the majority of the working class finally gained the vote.[30] It seems reasonable to suppose that the new voters were more amenable to mobilisation by the Labour Party than by the Liberals, but this cannot be tested adequately using the available electoral data. Once the constraints of the war and of the coupon election were gone, Labour did quite well. From 22 per cent of the vote and 63 seats (73 counting coalition Labour MPs) in 1918, Labour's gain of nearly 30 per cent of the vote and 142 seats in 1922 provides some support for the argument that the new electorate swung to Labour and that this led to the end of the Liberals as a viable force.

*Socio-economic change*

A third explanation for the decline of the Liberal Party, championed by many Marxian and Weberian sociologists, is that changes took place in Britain's *social structure*. Changes in the structure of capitalism led class to replace religion as the primary basis of political alignment, leading inexorably to the rise of the class-based party and the demise of the party based on élite clique or religion.[31] This explanation sees a growing group of Labour supporters paralleling changes in rates of unionisation and a growing class consciousness. Labour's triumph over the Liberals is thus posited to be a product of economic development.

Although there is some evidence for this last hypothesis, especially in Lancashire, there is a lack of systematic evidence covering the whole of Britain. There is little sign that the organisational strength of the Labour party grew until 1914, that Labour successes in local elections presaged Labour's breakthrough in 1922, or that class consciousness grew with unionisation.[32] As an alternative hypothesis, Duncan Tanner suggests that voters in many hitherto Liberal constituencies abandoned that party's mainly moral platform in favour of Labour's more materialistic stance because Labour's position was 'more closely related ... to the dominant Tory political culture, and so could more clearly oppose it'.[33]

One other factor played a role in the decline in the number of Liberal supporters. In the late Victorian and Edwardian eras, Liberalism and Nonconformity were closely inter-related. The massive dislocations that followed from the large-scale industrialisation of the British war effort cut many of the ties between the working classes and their local chapels, such that, after the end of the war, religion in general became less important in the lives of the newly enfranchised voters. With the clergy no longer intervening as effectively in daily life as before, their political influence necessarily waned. Ross McKibbin sees the sudden rise in Conservative success in Scotland as closely tied to the equally sudden fall of religious activity.[34] The move of the Simonite Liberals in Scotland toward the Unionist position was possible only because anti-Unionist sentiment, strong in the years before the war, paled before distrust of the materialist demands being proclaimed by the trade unions.[35]

### *Beyond the usual suspects: a core–periphery explanation*

As none of these hypotheses directly examines the role of the core–periphery cleavage, this path of inquiry remains to be explored. If the Liberals were in the first instance a party of the periphery, as suggested by the anti-Anglican stance of the party and the issues that it championed in the pre-war years, then they would naturally be less successful when the core–periphery cleavage was less pervasive. Whatever impact the élite squabbles and the increased franchise had, the fact remains that, by 1922, the year that most of the Irish periphery left the United Kingdom, the party that had led Britain through the First World War was divided into three groups that, combined, won only 29 per cent of the vote. Labour had drawn even. Two years and two elections later, the Liberal vote had fallen to 18 per cent and in 1931 was down to less than nine per cent, divided between government and opposition. The party's share of the vote did not again reach ten per cent until 1964.

If the religious politics of the pre-war period were in their essence core–periphery politics, the decline in religious intensity may well be connected with a decline in core–periphery conflict. If the country became more homogeneous following the First World War, then core–periphery differences would have sought fewer outlets for expression. People would have felt less inspired to attend chapel to show their disdain for London, the Crown, and the Anglican Church. The moral underpinnings of the Liberal creed would also have been weakened by the move away from core–periphery confrontation, and the party would have been left with its material position on free trade. The defection of such prominent Liberal industrialists as Sir Alfred Mond, who created ICI, served as a Liberal Cabinet minister under Lloyd George, and ardently supported free trade,[36] suggests that the materialist aspect of Liberal ideology was an insufficient balance to the fear of the rising Labour Party. Thus, a decline in the importance of the core–periphery cleavage may have disrupted the role of religion as a means of social identity just as it destroyed the political and moral base of the Liberal Party.

## Electoral turbulence and the rise of Labour

The near-disappearance of the Liberal Party was coupled with the rise of Labour to the status of a major party. Labour brought a new kind of politics to the fore: class conflict. The importance of the Anglican–Nonconformist conflict, both as a defining characteristic of the main parties and as a topic for political debate, was rapidly transcended by questions of trade union power, nationalisation, and the degree to which government had the right and duty to redistribute income and guide private consumption. While the end of Labour's electoral pact with the Liberals did not immediately cause a rise in Labour's organisational strength or electoral support, signs of the new electoral alignment were apparent as early as

1918. The surge occurred primarily in areas of England where large groups of unskilled workers with a culture of mutual support could be organised easily: coal mining areas. Although it could not have been predicted in 1918, Labour formed its first (coalition) government only five years later.

Labour did not represent the same interests as the Liberals had. The new party's success suggests strongly that the old core–periphery conflict was resolved, or at least almost completely overtaken by the new divide. Regression analysis of socio-economic, religious, and regional influences on the Conservative vote show only one region – Wales – where Conservative support was significantly below expectations.[37] At the same time, however, Labour took root fastest in counties far from London – in the periphery. The West Riding of Yorkshire, Durham, industrial Wales, and Glasgow were the cradles of Labour success. Despite the horrible living conditions among the London working classes between the wars, Labour only once captured a majority of seats in the capital.

## POST-WAR ELECTORAL DEVELOPMENTS

The first four post-war elections – 1945 to 1955 – set the tone for the 'Westminster model' of a stable two-party system with government and opposition alternating fairly regularly between the two. By this time the Liberals had been reduced to a minor party: winning two per cent of the seats on nine per cent of the votes in 1945 and 1950, but less than one per cent of the seats on three per cent of the votes in 1951 and 1955. The focus of political debate was squarely on the materialist redistribution of the socialist agenda: nationalisation, the new National Health Service, housing provided by the state, and the proper place of unions in industrial society. There was no place for regional politics or party attachments rooted in religion rather than class;[38] in fact, the Liberal Party toyed with the idea of amalgamating with the Conservatives in an alliance against the 'Red Menace' that was Labour. The key political feature of this period was Butskellism, the general agreement between the main parties on the utility of Keynesian economics and central planning to ensure continued growth, and on important political issues such as the country's stance on race relations, immigration, housing, and education policy. At the same time, the 'uniform swing' was paramount: the whole country shifted a share of its support from one party to the other in a way that turned a small shift in national support into a large shift in parliamentary representation, thereby assuring strong yet responsive governments.

Beginning in 1959, however, some years before the Butskellite consensus fell apart, the 'uniform swing' no longer occurred: Scotland, Wales, and the north of England began to lean to Labour while Conservative support increased in the south-east. An urban–rural divide opened from 1964 onwards.[39] Despite pronouncements that 'the Liberal Party ought to die',[40] the party regained strength, winning seats in the Scottish Highlands and seeing its share of the vote slowly climb back over ten per cent and then, in February 1974, to 23 per cent of the British vote.

The process accelerated following the electoral growth of Scottish and Welsh nationalism, which began in the 1960s. In response to the Conservative victory at the 1979 election, several Labour leaders, led by Michael Foot, wanted to bring the party back to its socialist roots. In 1981, differences among party élites over nationalisation, nuclear disarmament, and European integration pushed Roy Jenkins, David Owen, William Rodgers, and Shirley Williams to abandon the Labour Party in favour of a centrist position which they hoped would be more appealing to the voters. These four ex-Cabinet ministers formed the Social Democratic Party (SDP), and 25 Labour MPs and one Conservative MP soon adopted that party label. The SDP quickly formed an alliance with the Liberals to boost the electoral hopes of a centrist road between Labour and the Conservatives which, they hoped, would replace Labour as the primary anti-Conservative party. These hopes have had a rough road, though; although the alliance won 25 per cent of the vote in the 1983 election, Labour has been slowly regaining its lost support and is widely expected to win the next general election.

One problem faced by the SDP–Liberal Alliance was the different positions of the parties along the core–periphery divide. Throughout their period in the wilderness, the Liberals championed the politics of the periphery, from a Scottish Parliament to proportional representation. However, there was little sense among the electorate that these issues were important. The SDP, being an offshoot of Labour, was primarily a party representing economic interests: a softer form of Labour's socialism. The Liberals were an extremely decentralised party at the local level, while the local branches of the SDP, true to their Labour roots, were far more responsive to instructions from party headquarters.[41] This reflected key differences in the parties' origins: one on the peripheral side of the core–periphery divide, and the other on the lower side of the class cleavage.

The 1970s saw a second change in the British political space. High inflation and a severe economic crisis caused by the oil shocks brought to power a person and a party committed to reducing the welfare state and slashing government spending. Spending controls that were put into place by this Conservative government did more to centralise power than any previous administration had done this century. As a result, local government lost power throughout Britain. While the Conservatives suffered at the local level all over the country, the effects and repercussions were felt most in Scotland, where a long tradition of local government under union with England was undermined and support for independence rose from 24 per cent of the population in 1981 to 39 per cent in 1992.[42] The centralisation culminated in the Poll Tax fiasco, where the Scots were used as guinea pigs for all of Britain,[43] following which Margaret Thatcher was heard to say that the Scots should feel privileged that they were being subsidised by the 'marvellously tolerant English'.[44] Can it surprise anyone that the Scots, at least, did not take well to this treatment?

Between 1959 and 1987 the net effect of the north–south and urban–rural divides, and the formation of the SDP, has been to increase Labour's share of the two-party vote by 10.2 per cent in Scotland, and to increase the Conservative's share by 5.5 per cent in the south-east. During the same period the Liberals, with their SDP allies, have seen a major resurgence in support. A minor reversal of these trends in 1992 – a narrowing of the regional divide – have not been sufficient to allow either major party to claim to have general support from all parts of Great Britain. From its nadir in 1945, the north–south divide has increased to surpass even the divide that prevailed in the Edwardian elections of 1910 (Figure 2.2).

Given the great changes engendered in British politics by

FIGURE 2.2
CONSERVATIVE STRENGTH IN NORTH AND SOUTH, 1955–92

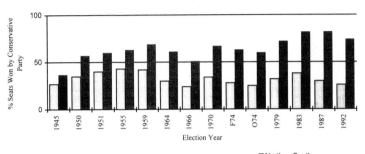

Sources: F. W. S. Craig, *British Parliamentary Election Results 1951–1973*, 2nd edition (Colchester: Parliamentary Research Services, 1983); I. Crewe, *British Parliamentary Constituencies, 1955–1974*, Machine-Readable file (Colchester: ESRC Archive number 661, 1977); I. McAllister and R. Rose, *United Kingdom Ecological Data 1983, 1987*, Machine-Readable file (Colchester: ESCR Archive number 2081, 1987); A. H. Wood and R. Wood (eds), *The Times Guide to the House of Commons April 1992* (London: Times Books, 1992).

the apparent resolution of religious differences and the rise of collectivism, it would be surprising if the divide were more than coincidence. Too much has changed for religion to be a deciding influence on the British party system. Nevertheless, there does seem to be a more than coincidental similarity between the geography of electoral support in the pre-war period and the geography that applies today. If we examine the geography of competition more closely, we may find reason to conclude that contemporary British politics are divided by the same core–periphery cleavage that affected politics at the turn of the century.

CONTINUITY AND CHANGE IN PARTY SUPPORT, 1885–1992

The foregoing discussion has divided Britain into two distinct areas for the general analysis of party fortunes. The south, defined as London, the south-east, and the Midlands, represents the heart of the country and the core of Britain's political and economic space. The north, meaning the north of England, Scotland, Wales, and the south-west peninsula of Devon and Cornwall, represents conquered territory, the hinterland, the periphery. The Conservatives have long prospered in the core, while various anti-Conservative parties have generally done better in the periphery. Before we turn to an examination of this electoral geography and so delve into the origins and consequences of regional polarisation, a brief exploration of the parameters of electoral change is in order. This next section examines the stability of electoral support for the three main parties between 1885 and 1992, drawing on a division of Britain into 45 units with substantially identical boundaries over the 29 elections.[45] This provides greater accuracy for the investigation of continuity and change, but of necessity says nothing about the geography of support.

The discussion that follows focuses on the Conservative Party because that party has been the most stable force in British politics since 1885. The Conservatives have unfailingly been the party of the Monarchy, of imperialist Britain, of the owners of the means of industrial and agricultural production, and of the Established (Anglican) Church. The only major change in Conservative positions over the period is in the area of protectionism and trade. Whereas the issue disrupted the Conservative Party in the first decade of the twentieth century, with some supporters of Free Trade leaving the party for the Liberals, the party brought Britain into the European Community in 1973. More astonishingly, given the party's history, the Conservatives have advocated further reductions of trade barriers through the Uruguay Round of the GATT and the Common Agricultural Policy (CAP) of the European Union.

The other parties, by contrast, hardly represent a unified, unchanging opposition. The Liberals of the pre-war period championed Disestablishment and Nonconformity, Home Rule (devolution), Free Trade, a reduction of the powers and privileges of the landed aristocracy and the House of Lords, and the rights of the working class. The party opposed much of the expansion of the British Empire, and had to be dragged into countering German expansionism before and shortly after the outbreak of the Great War. While the first years of this century saw the Liberals in an electoral pact with Labour, by the early 1950s several constituency parties were allied with the Conservatives, especially in Huddersfield and rural Wales. The bulk of the party considered the socialism of the Labour Party its chief foe. Today, after having absorbed part of the Labour Party, the Social and Liberal Democrats (as they are now called) are again considering an alliance with Labour against the Conservative government.

Labour has had a more stable electoral base during its existence but, although a few Labour candidates stood before 1900, the party was founded only in that year and has been a major political force only since 1922. The short period of existence and its low level of electoral success in the first 30 years of democracy make it unsuitable for the long-term study that this approach takes. As for the nationalist parties in Scotland and Wales, there has been opposition to English rule dating back to Robert the Bruce in the fourteenth century, but formalised, party-based opposition dates only from the Second World War. Thus, while it is a simplification only to examine continuity in support for the Conservative Party, this examination provides the optimal foundation for tracing the major electoral cleavages in existence since 1885.

The varied electoral successes of each of these parties can better be understood when viewed through the core–periphery lens. The proposed alliance of the Liberal Party with the Conservatives in the 1950s was a reaction to the centralising, nationalising tendencies of Clement Attlee's Labour government and the feeling that the Conservatives would better fight to preserve local traditions.[46] Lloyd George's flirting with the Conservatives a generation earlier was also sparked by uncertainty about socialism. Labour's origins in the periphery reflected the economic structure of the country, and its recent adoption of policies favouring the periphery are reactions to the economic realities of power shifting increasingly to south-east England. The Conservatives, unlike the other players in the British party system, represent stability over the decades.

## Stability and change

An examination of Figure 2.3 shows that the period from 1885 to 1906 was one of considerable electoral turmoil. The split in the Liberal Party in 1886, the slow recovery by that party of the seats and votes it had lost to the Liberal Unionists, and the overwhelming Liberal landslide of 1906 all combined to create great instability in the share of votes won by the Conservative and Liberal Unionist Parties over the period. General geographic stability of voting patterns began in 1906 and continued at least until 1979, with minor shocks in 1918 and 1931. Since 1951 the correlation of the geographic distribution of a party's support at a general election with that party's support at the immediately preceding election has been high and quite stable, despite Labour's debacle in 1983 and the Liberals' unsteady national share of the vote.

It has been hypothesised elsewhere that, barring a realignment, the geographic distribution of party support should correlate highly with the distribution at other elections in close temporal proximity.[47] In periods of partisan alignment, electoral volatility tends to be low. The evidence for Britain is illustrated in Figure 2.3. Plotting the correlation coefficients of the geographic distribution of party support in one election over the distribution of support at the previous election reveals considerable stability in British elections since the mid-1920s. In fact, there has been no election since 1931 where different regions have rapidly shifted their allegiance or their vote to one or more new parties. Labour's breakthrough in 1945 was an incremental increase over the party's 1935 share. Similarly, the Conservative victories of 1979 and the landslide of 1983 both involved incremental increases over the previous election, and not the capturing of new territory where the party had not previously been successful.

The emergence of the north–south divide contradicts this stability until the *gradual* nature of the divide's appearance is accounted for. The Conservatives have slowly been driven

FIGURE 2.3
INTER-ELECTION STABILITY

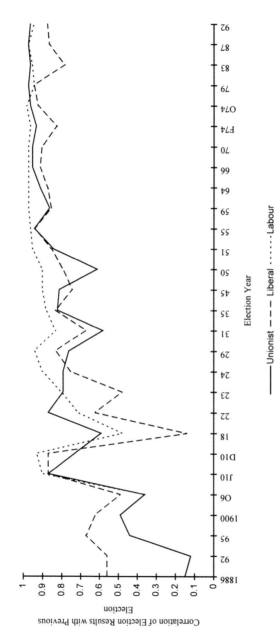

Election Year

——— Unionist – – – Liberal · · · · · · Labour

Correlation coefficients are obtained by dividing Britain into 45 units with stable boundaries over the period. These units are discussed in Bogdanor and Field, 'Lessons of History' (see note 45 below), with the exception of London which is divided into two units (north and south of the Thames), and Manchester set off from Lancashire. Data are taken from F.W.S. Craig, *British Parliamentary Election Results 1885–1918*, 2nd edition (Chichester: Parliamentary Research Services, 1989) and sources cited in Table 2.2.

out of Scotland since 1959, while they have just as slowly consolidated their hold on the south-east. The Liberal rise has been equally slow. The cumulative effect of regional electoral variation traced to the north–south divide between 1959 and 1987 was a two-party swing of 8.7 per cent to the Conservatives in the south (Greater London, the south-east and south-west) and two-party swings to Labour of 8.6 per cent in the north of England and 19.1 per cent in Scotland.[48] This is an average swing of slightly over one per cent per election for England, and three per cent for Scotland. The gradual, if not glacial, rate of change points to a slow exogenous trend affecting the electorate, not the immediate, abrupt impact of a particular issue, politician, or economic condition.

The argument that the national swing no longer holds may therefore be somewhat overstated. To be sure, the electorate does not swing from party to party as uniformly as in the 1950s, but the variation in inter-election swing is still far lower today than in the 1920s, or before the First World War. A more serious trend than volatility is the long-term, gradual shift in electoral support that has become known as the north–south divide.

Electorates are constantly changing. Even if each person never wavers in partisan support, the fact that people move house periodically means that a particular electoral constituency will not have exactly the same voters from election to election. Factors such as the rise of new towns, urban decay and suburban sprawl also cause a slow change in voters, to the extent that some electoral districts will shift their party loyalties over time. Voters and social circumstances change more the further one moves in time from a particular election. This process could be called the *decay of geographic alignment*. [49]

Correlating the geographic distribution of party support in various elections with support in a base election should show that elections that occur immediately before or after the base election will look more like that election than will elections that take place at more distant points in time. This relationship is celarly shown by plotting 29 British elections against the 1945 election, as in Figure 2.4. The thin, unbroken line in this figure plots the correlations of the Conservative/ Unionist share of the vote at the county level for each election between 1885 and 1992 with the party's county-level share of the vote in 1945. The elections of the 1930s were more like 1945 than were the elections of the 1920s, and the elections of the 1920s were more like 1945 than were the late nineteenth-century elections. Similarly, elections from the 1960s are less like 1945 than the elections of the 1950s. Similarity decreases the further each election is from 1945. The peak is in 1945: the geographic distribution of that election correlates with itself at a perfect 1.00.

It is apparent, from Figure 2.1, that the January 1910 election was the most geographically polarised of the eight pre-war elections, and, from Figure 2.2, that 1987 was the most polarised of the 14 post-war elections. Given the process of geographic alignment decay, one would expect that the spatial distribution of support at interwar elections would appear less like the January 1910 election than would the elections of 1900 and 1906, and that the post-war elections would look even less like 1910 than the inter-war ones (see the bold jagged line in Figure 2.4). However, this hypothesised relationship does not hold. The 1950 election is most divergent from that of January 1910, but elections after that date appear moderately more like 1910 than the elections of the 1930s and 1950s. To a limited extent, at least, the geographic pattern that characterised that first 1910 election reappears during the post-war period.

This counter-intuitive relation also holds when using 1987 as the base year. Elections that are in close temporal proximity are quite similar to 1987, with the similarity becoming less pronounced over time. This is consistent with Burnham's alignment theory. The declining trend stops in the 1920s, however, and the elections of 1910 and the early 1920s appear substantially more similar to 1987 than do the immediate post-war elections. The elections of the beginning of this century, especially 1910, are far more like contemporary elections in terms of the geographic distribution of support for the Conservative Party than would be expected, given the changes in the competing parties, the electoral system, and the issues under discussion that occurred during the mid-twentieth century.[50]

FIGURE 2.4
GEOGRAPHIC STABILITY OF CONSERVATIVE AND UNIONIST PARTY SUPPORT

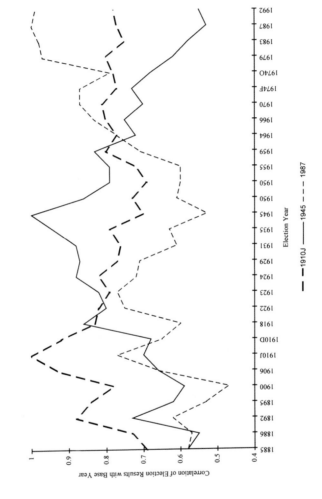

Source: See Figure 2.2.

## *The geography of support*

The geographic stability data presented in the previous section do not measure the north–south divide. Geographic similarity does not necessarily imply geographic polarisation. A rough way to capture the size of the north–south divide over time is to compare party support in the two parts of the country and to calculate thereby an index of polarisation. Analogous to the Alford index of class voting, the index of polarisation reports each party's share of the vote won in the south of the country, subtracted from the share won in the north. The index departs somewhat from the norm in that the sign of the relationship is important: a party with a positive value obtains a larger share of the vote in the periphery than in the core, while a party with a negative value captures more of the vote in the core. This departure is necessary to capture the changing nature of support for the Liberal Party as it gains increasing support from the core through loss of support to Scottish and Welsh nationalists. Of course, the index of polarisation does not control for the distribution of social class, religion, or other factors known to influence party loyalty, matters that will be discussed in later chapters, but it does give a broad measure of regional variation.

Figure 2.5 shows clearly how the fortunes of the three main parties have fluctuated over the years. Results for the Conservative and Unionist grouping are most informative, showing a moderate but increasing degree of geographic polarisation in the years leading up to and immediately following the Great War, with minimal polarisation in the 1940s and 1950s, and with a widening gap since 1959. The erosion of Conservative support in Scotland since 1974 emerges quite strongly as the most extreme amount of polarisation the party has experienced since the First World War. The changing geography of Conservative support is mapped for the elections of January 1910, 1951, and 1992 in Figure 2.6.

Evidence for the other parties is somewhat more complex. The Liberals began about as polarised as the Conservatives but toward the north. With the emergence of the Labour Party, Liberal polarisation decreased so that, by the end of the

FIGURE 2.5
DIFFERENCE IN PARTY SUPPORT BETWEEN NORTH AND SOUTH

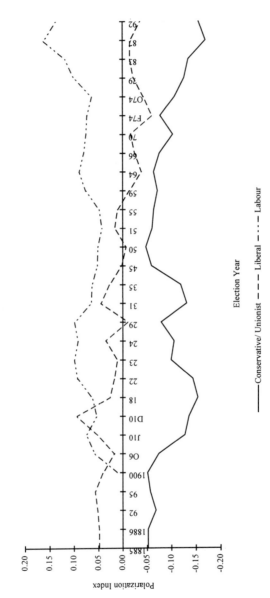

——— Conservative/ Unionist  – – – Liberal  –··– Labour

A positive value for the polarisation index signifies that the party received a larger share of the vote in the north of Britain (Scotland, Wales, and northern England) than in the south (London, the Home Counties, the south-west, and the Midlands), while a negative value signifies that it received a larger share of the southern vote than the northern vote.
Source: See Figure 2.2.

Second World War, the Liberals no longer showed the electoral bias that was the party's mainstay in the Edwardian period. From 1959 the Liberals emerged with a southern bias in response to a successful attempt by Jo Grimond to reposition the party to challenge the Conservatives in their heartland. Liberal support crept toward a balanced distribution during the 1970s following the success of Grimond's policies, reaching near parity due to the pooling of electoral fortunes with the new centrist Social Democratic Party (SDP) in 1983. With Labour recapturing in the two most recent elections most of the voters who defected, Liberal polarisation toward the south has again increased.

The origins of the Labour Party were in the mines and factories of Yorkshire, Wales, and Scotland, so its geographic polarisation was quite high at first. It then fell slowly over time as the party extended its support to southern cities through the 1950s, before rising again in the 1960s and 1970s. The sudden leap since 1979 can be traced in part to the same phenomenon that marks dramatic changes in Liberal polarisation: the creation of the SDP. Other factors influencing this were the electoral success of the Scottish nationalists (21 per cent of the Scottish vote in 1992) and the continued loss of support to the Conservatives in the south.

### CONCLUSION AND IMPLICATIONS

The British party system has undergone considerable change in the century since the third Reform Acts. The Liberals, briefly the dominant force in British politics, have recently recovered from near-oblivion to offer viable candidates in many constituencies throughout the country. Labour has emerged as the main alternative to the ever-dominant Conservatives. In line with the rise of Labour, the primary cleavage that shapes British politics has also changed from one based on core and periphery to one based on class.

Far from being 'frozen', the British party system has been evolving with the expansion of the electorate. Evolution has continued since the advent of universal suffrage too, with different cleavages coming into salience at different points in time. Parties have gained and lost general electoral strength, and have shifted their geographic strongholds from region to region in Britain. The Westminster model of party stability has held only for a very short period.

Despite the high degree of instability that has characterised the British party system there is sufficient evidence to suggest that the similarity in the electoral geography of Britain between the core–periphery alignment of the Edwardian period and in the north–south divide of today is greater than would be expected. This finding provides initial support for the hypothesis that undergirds this study: *that a core–periphery cleavage has re-emerged to influence British politics after lying dormant for the period immediately before and after the Second World War.*

Given the preliminary support for the hypothesis, an important question emerges: has the socio-economic base of the Conservative Party changed over time? Given the constancy of the party's position on various issues, the improbability of such a change would raise the likelihood that the distribution of electoral support would depend on external factors embedded in Britain's social geography. A change in social geography would affect electoral geography, perhaps with the regional effect found above.

The immediate relationship between social geography and political geography can be examined through the two bodies of theory examined in Chapter One. If either or both of these approaches are sufficient to explain the changing regional patterns of the British case, then there is no need to introduce a core–periphery analysis. If, however, they are found to be insufficient without an explicit and theoretically grounded regional component, then the examination of core and periphery that begins in Chapter Four and continues through Chapter Five offers an alternative path for explanation. We now turn to an examination of alternative theoretical approaches.

FIGURE 2.6
CONSERVATIVE (CONSERVATIVE/UNIONIST) ELECTORAL SUPPORT

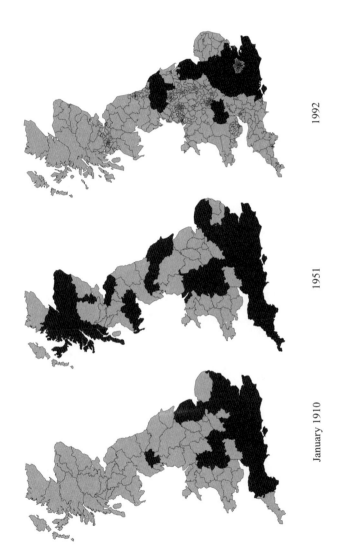

January 1910

1951

1992

NOTES

1. C. S. Seymour, *Electoral Reform in England and Wales: The Development of the Parliamentary Franchise 1832–1885* (New Haven: Yale University Press, 1915); *Census of the United Kingdom, 1911* (London: HMSO, 1912).

2. H. J. Hanham, *Elections and Party Management: Politics in the Time of Disraeli and Gladstone* (London: Longman, 1959) p. xvii; D. E. D. Beales, *The Political Parties of Nineteenth Century Britain* (London: Historical Association, 1971); S. Beer, *Modern British Politics: Parties and Pressure Groups in the Collectivist Age* (New York: W. W. Norton, 1982).

3. L. Stephen, 'On the Choice of Representation by Popular Constituencies', *Essays on Reform* (London, 1867) pp. 106–7.

4. Quoted in N. Gash, *Politics in the Age of Peel*, 2nd ed. (Hassocks: Harvester, 1977) pp. xxiv–v. Italics in original.

5. In many others the landlord desperately wanted to retain control, not necessarily with success. In a rather extreme example, J.W.E. Erle Drax, Member for Wareham (Dorset), gave the following speech: 'Electors of Wareham! I understand that some evil-disposed person has been circulating a report that I wish my tenants, and other persons dependent on me, to vote according to their conscience. This is a dastardly lie; calculated to injure me. I wish, and I intend, that these persons shall vote for me.' Quoted in Hanham, p. 52.

6. Seymour, p. 281.

7. Martin Pugh suggests that 1880 marks the first *general* election in Britain because, among other things, five-sixths of the constituencies were actually contested. See M. Pugh, *The Making of Modern British Politics*, 2nd ed. (Oxford: Blackwell, 1993) p. 3.

8. G. J. Holyoake, *Working-Class Representation* (Birmingham: 1868). Quoted in Hanham, p. xii.

9. *Aberdare Times*, 14 November 1868. Quoted in K.O. Morgan, *Wales in British Politics 1868–1922* (Cardiff: University of Wales Press, 1970) p. v. On David Lloyd George's political memories, see K.O. Morgan, *David Lloyd George 1863–1945* (Cardiff: University of Wales Press, 1981) p. 11.

10. M. Ostrogorski, *Democracy and the Organisation of Political Parties* (London, Haskell House, 1902, reprinted 1970) pp. 90–3.

11. W.E. Gladstone, *A Chapter of Autobiography*, 2nd ed. (London, 1868) p. 11. Gladstone's 1863 comments can be found in Ostrogorski, *Democracy and the Organisation of Political Parties*, p. 91.

12. To consolidate their position in society, many of the landed Puritan élite joined the Church of England in the years after the English Civil War. All of their dependents, from servants to farmers to tradesmen, tended to follow them. See H. Perkin, *The Origin of Modern British Society, 1780–1880* (London: Routledge & Kegan Paul, 1969) pp. 34–5; E.S. Wellhofer, *Democracy, Capitalism and Empire in Late Victorian Britain* (London: Macmillan, 1996) p. 12.

13. N. Blewett, *The Peers the Parties, and the People* (London: Macmillan, 1972) p. 4.

14. The Irish Nationalists supported the Liberals on most major issues. Although they never formally entered the government, Irish votes maintained the Liberal government majority between December 1910 and the creation of the coalition government in 1915.

15. K. Wald, *Crosses on the Ballot: Patterns of British Voter Alignment Since 1885* (Princeton: Princeton University Press, 1983) pp. 122–61; E.S. Wellhofer, (1996).

16. W.L. Miller, *Electoral Dynamics in Britain Since 1918* (London: Macmillan, 1977) pp. 4–5; Wald.

17. Letter dated 16 January 1896 quoted in K. O. Morgan (ed.), *Lloyd George Family Letters 1885–1936* (Cardiff: University of Wales Press and London: Oxford University Press, 1973) p. 94.
18. A. Marr, *The Battle for Scotland* (London: Penguin Books, 1992).
19. Quoted in W.L. Miller and G. Raab, 'The Religious Alignment at English Elections Between 1918 and 1970', *Political Studies*, 25, 2 (June 1977) p. 229.
20. Quoted in Blewett, pp. 345–6.
21. J.A. Hobson, 'The General Election: A Sociological Interpretation', *The Sociological Review*, 32 (April 1910) pp. 112–13. Hobson was not completely accurate, however. Warwickshire and Staffordshire formed part of 'producer's England' and yet, in 1910, much of this region behaved politically as if it were part of 'consumer's England' thanks to the continued influence of the Liberal Unionist leader Joseph Chamberlain and his Birmingham electoral machine. This exception only highlights the general accuracy of his statement.
22. See above.
23. H.N. Brailsford, *The War of Steel and Gold* (London: G. Bell & Sons, 1914).
24. Grey of Falloden, *Twenty-Five Years* (London, 1925), Vol. II, p. 306. Quoted in M. Howard, *War and the Liberal Conscience* (Oxford: Oxford University Press, 1989) pp. 73–4.
25. Ibid., p. 11.
26. Diary entry by the Liberal MP Maurice (later Baron) Hankey, quoted in C. Cook, *A Short History of the Liberal Party* (New York: St. Martin's Press, 1976) p. 67.
27. J. M. Keynes, *The Economic Consequences of the Peace* (London: Macmillan, 1919) p. 133.
28. Andrew Bonar Law manuscript collection, House of Lords, 1918. Quoted in V. Bogdanor, 'Electoral Pacts in Britain Since 1886', in D. Kavanagh (ed.), *Electoral Politics* (Oxford: Clarendon Press, 1992) p. 176.
29. The coupon was a letter, signed by Lloyd George and Bonar Law on behalf of the coalition government, that the candidate had the full support of the coalition. Many candidates, from all three parties – Liberals, Conservatives, and Labour – were given the coupon, while other candidates, from the same parties, were not. The attempt to divide the electorate along cross-party lines makes the societal base of party support for this election particularly hard to evaluate.
30. C. Matthew, R. McKibbin, and J. Kay, 'The Franchise Factor in the Rise of the Labour Party', *English Historical Review*, 91, 361 (October 1976) pp. 723–52.
31. This is the essence of the political modernisation argument. See S.M. Lipset and S. Rokkan, 'Cleavage Structures, Party Systems, and Voter Alignments: An Introduction', in S.M. Lipset and S. Rokkan (eds), *Party Systems and Voter Alignments* (New York: The Free Press, 1967) for a general discussion of this. J.F. Glaser, 'English Nonconformity and the Decline of Liberalism', *American Historical Review*, 63, 2 (January 1958) pp. 352–63; D. E. Butler and D. Stokes, *Political Change in Britain*, 2nd edition (London: Macmillan, 1974) pp. 109–21; and P. F. Clarke, *Lancashire and the New Liberalism* (Cambridge: Cambridge University Press, 1971) detail the British case.
32. D. Tanner, *Political Change and the Labour Party 1900–1918* (Cambridge: Cambridge University Press, 1990) pp. 8–9.
33. Ibid., p. 421.
34. R. McKibbin, 'Class and the Conventional Wisdom: The Conservative Party and the "Public" in Inter-war Britain', in R. McKibbin, *The Ideologies of Class: Social Relations in Britain 1880–1950* (Oxford: Oxford University Press, 1991)

pp. 284–5.

35. In 1930 John Maynard Keynes wrote that 'I am sure that a very great many members of the public ... think ... that Labour is greedy and is asking for a larger and larger share of a smaller product, and we are getting nearer and nearer to the abyss' (private session of the Macmillan committee, 22 October 1930, quoted in ibid., p. 284).
36. Ibid., p. 283.
37. Miller, p. 181.
38. This is not strictly true: a Scottish Nationalist won a by-election in the waning days of the Second World War, and the 'Scottish Convention' agitated for a Scottish parliament between 1945 and 1950. However, the nationalist lost his seat in the 1945 general election, and the agitation faded after the three larger parties failed to embrace the cause. For a discussion, see Marr, pp. 95–102.
39. J. Curtice and M. Steed, 'Electoral Choice and the Production of Government: The Changing Operation of the Electoral System in the United Kingdom Since 1955', *British Journal of Political Science*, 12, 3 (July 1982) pp. 249-98; J. Curtice and M. Steed, 'Proportionality and Exaggeration in the British Electoral System,' *Electoral Studies*, 5, 3 (December 1986) pp. 209–28.
40. *The Times*, Leader, 12 May 1964. Quoted in W. Wallace, 'Survival and Revival', in V. Bogdanor (ed.), *Liberal Party Politics* (Oxford: Clarendon Press, 1983) p. 43.
41. J. Stevenson, *Third Party Politics Since 1945: Liberals, Alliance and Liberal Democrats* (Oxford: Blackwell, 1993) p. 79.
42. J. Mitchell and L. G. Bennie, 'Thatcherism and the Scottish Question', in C. Rallings, D. M. Farrell, D. Denver, and D. Broughton (eds), *British Elections and Parties Yearbook 1995* (London: Frank Cass, 1996) pp. 94–5.
43. D. Butler, A. Adonis, and T. Travers, *Failure in British Government: The Politics of the Poll Tax* (Oxford: Oxford University Press, 1994).
44. *Daily Express*, 25 April 1990, quoted in Mitchell and Bennie, p. 94.
45. These 45 units are based loosely on English counties and Welsh and Scottish regions. The difficulty of building them, given the radical county-level boundary changes in 1971, are explored in V. Bogdanor and W.H. Field, 'Lessons of History: Core and Periphery in British Electoral Behaviour, 1910–1992', *Electoral Studies*, 12, 3 (September 1993) pp. 204–24.
46. During the late 1940s, the Conservatives made much of Labour's transfer of power from private industry to Whitehall and the reduction of local control that resulted. The loss of local control that resulted from the Conservative reorganisation of local government in the 1970s and the reduction of its spending powers and freedom of manoeuvre in the 1980s were far higher than that created by nationalisations. For discussions, see W.L. Miller, *The End of British Politics? Scots and English Political Behaviour in the Seventies* (Oxford: Clarendon Press, 1981) pp. 19–26.
47. W.D. Burnham, *Critical Elections and the Mainsprings of American Politics* (New York: W.W. Norton, 1970); W.D. Burnham, 'Realignment Lives: The 1994 Earthquake and its Implications', in C. Campbell and B. Rockman, *The Clinton Presidency: First Appraisals* (Chatham, NJ: Chathman House, 1996) pp. 363–96.
48. J. Curtice and M. Steed, 'The Results Analysed', in D. Butler and D. Kavanagh, *The British General Election of 1987* (London: Macmillan, 1988) p. 330.
49. According to estimates from the British Election Studies, some 15 to 25 per cent of voters change their party choice from one election to the next. Over the course of several succeeding elections, say from 1979 to 1992, the number who change is likely to be much higher, perhaps as high as 30 to 40 per cent.

Once the effect of migration is considered, it becomes easy to see how the geographic dimensions of a particular electoral alignment might decay. For a discussion of mobility and volatility, see W. H. Field, 'Electoral Volatility and the Structure of Competition: A Reassessment of Voting Patterns in Britain 1959–1992', *West European Politics*, 17, 4 (October 1994) pp. 149–65.

50. All of the correlation coefficients in this table are skewed upward by the limited number of cases involved (45). The need to create a data set of surrogate counties with common boundaries across time necessitated combining many constituencies into each unit. This naturally decreased the heterogeneity of the population and affected the coefficients. An analysis of 104 units using only the elections between 1885 and 1979 with 1979 as the base year showed a pattern similar to the one discussed in the body of the text, but with lower correlation coefficients.

# CHAPTER THREE

# Current Explanations for Regional Change: A Critical Evaluation

INTEREST IN the north–south divide is rather high in Britain. Many political scientists and sociologists have grappled with the question of what is happening to British parties and how the geographic changes described in Chapter Two affect British politics. Some say Britain is undergoing a major transformation of its political system and that this has made the electoral system less responsive to changes in public opinion.[1] They maintain that, despite the current public repudiation of the Conservative Party, the end result of the divide will be Conservative rule for years to come. Others say that nothing at all is happening that cannot be explained through short-term factors, such as leader popularity, and that these effects are just as likely to be reversed tomorrow as to continue.[2] Still others trace the emergence of the divide to concrete changes in social structure and regional economic performance or to perceptions about that performance.[3] A fourth group sees the origins of the divide in rising nationalism in the Celtic periphery of the country.[4] This chapter examines these competing explanations for geographic polarisation with a view to showing that the answers offered so far are radically incomplete.

Explanations for the north–south divide have generally fallen into two camps. Social identity models are predicated on group memberships and partisan loyalty. Economic voting models are based on voter evaluations of the party choices and making a fresh decision at each election. As such, they

64

have generally fallen into two categories: structural change and economic performance. Changes in either the class structure or in the regional state of the economy are obvious candidates for sources of regional variation, but, as will be shown below, such changes are not in themselves sufficient as explanations.

Economic performance, or at least individual perceptions of performance, locate the cause of the north–south divide in the economic theory of voting. This theory has two relevant branches. The first relates electoral change to local variations in economic performance. This category reflects *objective* economic interests such as unemployment or house price increases. The second relates the divide to regional variations in perceptions of well-being, the reasoning being that the voters' *subjective* impressions of personal or national success are much more important than concrete evidence of economic health or stagnation. A discussion of each of these categories is presented below, outlining the thrust of each argument before offering a critique showing the weaknesses of the approaches under discussion.

### A COMMON BASE

Nearly all researchers agree that certain factors have influenced voting preferences in Britain. On both aggregate and individual levels, evidence has shown that occupation and housing tenure (whether the voter lives in owner-occupied or public housing) provide the best predictors for voter choice. While the debate over how to operationalise the complexities of class has raged, there was general agreement through the 1960s that the British electoral experience was of a class-bound electorate feeding instinc-tively into class-based parties. Although the Westminster model of two-party politics dates only from the Second World War, the traditional view focused on its simple mechanisms of class representation and governmental accountability as the way politics should be and would be for some time to come. Elections were framed as two-party contests, decided by national shifts in party support among the small group of floating voters.[5] As such, the class base of the British party system represented something of a paradigm.

To be sure, there were regional variations in party support in the 1960s. Dividing the country into two regions (Lancashire, Yorkshire, the north of England, Scotland, and Wales versus the south-east, south-west, and the Midlands), Butler and Stokes found that, in the north, working-class support for the Conservatives equalled middle-class support for Labour, whereas in the south, working-class Tories were more prevalent than middle-class socialists.[6] The authors conceded that there were historical and economic differences between the attributes of these two areas, most notably in the scale and type of industrialisation and in the history of economic difficulties since 1918, but they placed most of their emphasis on the principle that a dominant party attracts additional support through a 'concentration effect,' which exaggerates that party's vote beyond its 'natural level' and homogenises local opinions. This effect comes from two different sources: the first being a perception-based mechanism wherein voters evaluate the political feel of their neighbourhood, ward, or constituency and come to identify with it,[7] and the second being the long-term processes of political socialisation whereby children maintain the political attitudes of their parents against a changing objective background.[8] Added to this was the possibility that local party organisations were more active in areas of high support, magnifying the electoral result.[9]

The first approach we shall examine is the possibility that there is no divide exclusive of socio-economic change. This is the structural explanation of electoral behaviour. We shall then turn to the influence of short-term economic changes, following the economic or rational model of voting.

## SOCIO-ECONOMIC EXPLANATIONS: NO NORTH–SOUTH DIVIDE

An important explanation of the north–south divide is a change in the social structure that alters the composition of the electorate in each constituency. In the United States, gentrification has transformed parts of some cities from semi-slums occupied by indigent minorities to exclusive residential neighbourhoods occupied by upwardly mobile people, with concurrent changes in political colour. A similar thing has happened Britain. Areas in some cities have been rejuvenated (the most famous being perhaps the Canary Wharf project in East London, where derelict dockland has been turned into an expensive centre for residential and office space), while other areas have become newly derelict as coal seams have been exhausted and miners have moved away. On a larger scale, the economic boom in the south-east in the last decade has created many managerial and financial service jobs, while economic troubles in the country's industrial sector have eliminated many blue collar, unskilled manual jobs. The socio-economic structure of the country has changed, both nationally (more middle class than before) and regionally (the new middle class is more concentrated in certain areas). As reported in the census, manual workers[10] fell from 62 to 30 per cent of the economically active population between 1951 and 1991, while the share of professional and managerial positions more than doubled (see Table 3.1). The numbers of self-employed people also increased sharply. Findings from the British Election Studies (BES) suggest that these changes cost the Labour Party 4.5 per cent of the electorate between 1964 and 1987.[11] This loss would be distributed unevenly around the country, with the impact on the vote distributed commensurably.

McAllister and Studlar tested the hypothesis that changes

TABLE 3.1
DISTRIBUTION OF THE ECONOMICALLY ACTIVE AND EMPLOYED
POPULATION BY OCCUPATIONAL CATEGORY, 1951–91

|  | 1951 | 1961 | 1971 | 1981 | 1991 |
|---|---|---|---|---|---|
| Employers/Self-employed | 6.7 | 6.4 | 6.5 | 6.4 | 12.5 |
| Professionals/Managers | 12.0 | 14.3 | 19.1 | 24.8 | 28.4 |
| Clerical/Sales | 16.3 | 18.6 | 19.5 | 19.3 | 21.6 |
| Supervisors/Foremen | 2.6 | 2.9 | 3.9 | 4.2 | 7.9 |
| Manual | 62.3 | 57.7 | 51.1 | 45.4 | 29.6 |

Sources: A.F. Heath and S.-K. McDonald, 'Social Change and the Future of the Left', *Political Quarterly*, 58, 4 (October–December 1987) pp. 364–77; OPCS, *Census of the United Kingdom, 1991* (London: HMSO, 1994).

in occupational structure of constituencies and regions account for territorial polarisation.[12] By combining ecological data from the 1981 census with BES data on current occupation, political attitudes, family background, local economic expectations, and established local political traditions, the authors were able to examine individual behaviour within the context of the social structure of the region of residence. For the purposes of this analysis, the authors divided Britain into six regions: the south (outside London), London, the Midlands, the north, Wales, and Scotland, and used dummy variables to compare behaviour in the last five regions to the most Conservative south. For 1979, with no controls, voting behaviour in all five regions appeared to be statistically distinct from behaviour in the south, but this difference disappeared in all cases except Wales after adding controls for social structure to the model. For 1983 and 1987, the north, Wales, and Scotland all showed statistically significant differences from the south, even after taking into account constituency-level differences in social structure, but these differences were only half of what they appeared to be before adding the constituency data to the model.[13]

The authors then explored several alternative explanations for the regional polarisation: spatially distinct political attitudes, regional variation in party leader popularity, constituency-level socio-economic effects, voters' personal evaluations of economic conditions (for 1987), and variations in party strength. Regional differences in political attitudes toward socialism (measured by a 'feeling' scale in the BES) explained part of the polarisation, and the other variables explained much of the rest. After these categories of variables were added to the models, only Wales stood out as a distinct region in 1979 and 1987, while Scotland alone stood out in 1983. Examining the coefficients of their equations, McAllister and Studlar concluded that 86 per cent of the regional variation in voting behaviour in 1979 could be explained through variations in social composition while the remaining variation could be explained through the distribution of political attitudes. For 1983 and 1987 the respective numbers are 69.5 and 72 per cent, explained through the standard variables available in survey and ecological data.[14]

There are a few problems with this study, however. First, as the authors admit, using variations in political attitudes as an explanation for variations in voting begs the question of what the source of that variation might be. Eighteen to 28 per cent of the regional polarisation has been 'explained' through the distribution of political attitudes, but political attitudes and voting tendencies have a similar source, and they tend to go hand-in-hand.[15] Does not spatial variation in political attitudes itself reflect the north–south divide?

The influence of party leaders and local party dominance is more problematic: the Labour leaders in 1983 and 1987 were both Welsh, yet McAllister and Studlar found that their popularity in Scotland relative to the south of England explained 14 per cent of the mean regional deviation in 1987. Is this not also an effect of region in its core–periphery guise? If a core–periphery cleavage is influencing the spatial distribution of party support, this would explain why popularity of a Labour leader from the periphery is higher in the periphery. The same criticism can be levelled at the variable for local party dominance, with 11 per cent of the variance explained for 1983: what is the source of this local strength independent of social structure or cleavage system?

Table 3.2 replicates elements of McAllister and Studlar's Table 7, showing how much of the regional electoral polarisation has actually been explained. A considerable part of the apparent regional polarisation is indeed a product of the uneven distribution of unionisation, housing tenure, social class, and political socialisation from one's parents, but not all can be explained this way. Voters with the same socio-economic and structural characteristics do not vote the same way across the country. In 1987, for example, a voter outside the south was 12.4 per cent more likely to vote Labour than an identical voter living in the Home Counties, even after all controls for socio-economic status were applied. Removing all these non-structural explanations for regional variation, one finds the model explains 75 per cent of the regional variation in Conservative support (mean regional deviation from the south of England) in 1979, but only 66 per cent in 1983 and 63 per cent in 1987. This is a widening regional divide.

TABLE 3.2
PATTERNS AND COMPONENTS OF REGIONAL VOTING, 1979–87

| Mean regional deviation from the south of England (outside London) | 1979 | 1983 | 1987 |
|---|---|---|---|
| Without controls | 22.6 | 26.4 | 28.6 |
| With all controls | 4.2 | 2.8 | 3.0 |
| With exogenous controls only | 8.8 | 10.8 | 12.4 |

Source: Calculated from I. McAllister and D. Studlar, p. 190. Exogenous controls include parental partisanship, father's occupation, socio-economic status (education, occupation, and unemployment), economic life-style (housing tenure, income, and trade union membership) ascribed characteristics (age, gender, and race), and constituency class composition. Other controls include political attitudes, attitudes toward the party leaders, retrospective economic evaluation, and local party dominance.

## Migration

A second hypothesis concerns the effects of migration on the geographic distribution of party support. Migration in the United States has been shown to smooth regional differences in partisanship; Republicans moving south have brought their party with them.[16] As for Britain, social and geographic mobility have both increased since the 1940s; people are far more willing to move great distances for a job today than their grandparents were. This raises the possibility that workers are moving to regions that they find more politically and socially amenable: white collar Conservative workers from the north of England are moving south in search of employment, while (less plausibly) Labour-supporting manual workers are moving north. If this is the case, then the changes in social geography should magnify the spatial polarisation of electoral support by homogenising different regions toward different parties.

This hypothesis has been found to be incorrect. Migration over long distances took place predominantly among middle-class, Conservative-leaning voters, no matter what their regional origin and destination was, leading to a migration-based *reduction* in the north–south divide of less than 0.5 per cent.[17] An analysis of the British Election Study found that voters who moved across the north–south boundary tended to adopt the partisan disposition of the neighbourhood and region into which they moved.[18] Middle-class Labour supporters who moved south became Conservative converts. The move had a negligible impact on the north–south divide as migration itself and the conversion of migrants tended to cancel each other out.

## Unexplained polarisation

Work relating socio-economic change as measured through the censuses of 1981 and 1991 to voting changes between 1979 and 1992 shows that such changes can indeed, account for some of the north–south divide. At the constituency level, structural changes in class structure and housing tenure, and non-structural changes in unemployment patterns can account for about half of the net swing to the Conservatives in the south and to Labour in the north.[19] However, accounting for half the divide in terms of structural change does not explain it in its entirety; there remains a large residual regional change whose origins have not yet been found.

### ECONOMIC EXPLANATIONS

While it impossible to cover all aspects of economics and voting here, it is necessary to review and analyse some of the literature to set the context against which the core–periphery model is to be placed.[20] With this in mind, the next section lays out some of the essentials of the individual- and regional-level economic models.

It has long been hypothesised that there is a link between economics and voting. As early as 1814, Lord Brougham wrote that 'a government is not supported a hundredth part so much by the constant, uniform, quiet prosperity of the country as by those damnable spurts which Pitt used to have just in the nick of time'.[21] People vote to maximise their personal gain, or, put more precisely, to maximise their (predominantly economic) utility. In the case of Britain, members of the working class broadly, but not uniformly, favour the Labour Party's programmes of nationalisation, full employment, and the expansion of the welfare state as being in their interests. The middle class, the petite bourgeoisie, and other groups oppose nationalisation as an attack on their wealth and social status while favouring the Conservative Party's economic policies of *laissez-faire* capitalism and low inflation as more suited to their interests. Economic policy has provoked sharp conflict between the parties and has provided a way for voters to distinguish one from another since the protectionism versus free trade disputes in the first years of this century.[22]

The details of economic policy are a series of trade-offs. While all voters prefer good times over bad times, choices between inflation and unemployment (if such choices truly exist), between nationalisation and privatisation, and between an expanding or contracting welfare state, are not so clear cut. Commentators and politicians have both interpreted voter choices and opinion poll results as reflecting mandates for the policies of the winning party (prospective voting) or as judgements of the effects of past policies (retrospective voting). Retrospective models of party support (reward–punishment models) hypothesise that vote preference depends at least in part upon the aggregate economic performance of some prior period, while prospective models (issue priority models) suggest that voters choose between the parties' competing promises.

## Single-election studies

Many studies have found that party popularity is affected by aggregate economic performance. As recession hits, the government usually finds itself trailing the opposition in the beauty contest that is the opinion-polling industry, while rapid growth with low inflation and interest rates is almost a sure sign of excellent re-election chances. If economic performance has such an effect on party popularity, it makes sense that the effect should vary as objective and subjective economic conditions vary across a country. Voters are aware of national economic statistics through the prominence given to the economy in the national media.[23] They are also aware of conditions in their immediate surroundings, as measured by such indicators as the number of houses up for sale and the level of local unemployment. If economic conditions affect voting, then local economic conditions should affect voting as well, if only in the immediate locale. Some of the tests of the economic voting model have considered this regional variation.

John Owens and Larry Wade added a specifically regional component, distance from London, to constituency-level data covering unemployment and wage increases for predicting the vote in 1983.[24] They found that regional economic variation was a useful variable for predicting the 1983 election outcome but that the geographic component existed in addition to regional variations in objective economic conditions. They offered no explanation of why distance from London should be an important predictor over and above local economic performance, however.

The Conservative vote in the 1987 election was not as closely related to immediate economic performance as it seems to have been in 1983.[25] Eight years of Thatcherism had changed the economic map of Britain, but not enough to explain the divergence between local economic performance and party support: changes in electoral outcomes made for a rather smooth continuation of trends that the authors dated to 1959. Measures of prosperity and unemployment sometimes conflicted strongly with the electoral outcome; in urban areas, for example, the Conservative vote fell, but by no more than elsewhere in the country.[26]

Of the other major studies of economics and voting, most are limited by the short period under study. In perhaps the most famous example, Goodhart and Bhansali produced an elegant unemployment- and inflation-driven model of government popularity in Britain which failed miserably immediately after publication when the 1969–70 economic boom failed to secure the Labour government's re-election.[27]

## Multi-election studies

Regional-level examinations of multiple elections are rare. The ones that exist are as inconclusive as are the single-election studies. Detailed analyses relating constituency-level electoral change between 1979 and 1987 to regional variations in voters' perceptions of their personal economic situation over the period appear to support a connection between perceptions and party support.[28] In the latter two elections, people who thought their personal economic situation had improved over the prior year tended to vote Conservative, while people who thought their personal economic situation had deteriorated tended to vote Labour or Liberal. Perceptions were most negative in the north of England, Wales, and Scotland during the 1980s, where the economy was lagging, and were most favourable in the booming south-east. The situation was reversed in 1979, with Labour as the incumbent government and the economic picture less lopsided. Noting regional variations in levels of economic satisfaction, Johnston and his colleagues concluded that perceptions of economic conditions led to the increase in the north–south divide in the 1980s.

The influence of perceptions is problematic, however. While perceptions are naturally important in making decisions, they are influenced a great deal by preconceptions. In particular, people who support the governing party are likely to look favourably on its economic performance and conclude that their personal situation has improved (or that the other party would have done worse). Not everybody will do this, of course, but it is apparent that the arrow of causation between perceptions and party choice does not necessarily flow in only one direction. Dalton quotes an American voter who denies being guided by partisanship: 'I vote for the candidate and not the party. It just seems like the Democrats always choose the best candidate.'[29] As Norpoth concludes, the filter of partisanship 'makes it possible to concentrate on those aspects of the record that allows [*sic*] one to feel satisfied or dissatisfied, depending on whether one's party is in power or not.'[30]

Time-series analyses of government popularity in the early 1980s partially disaggregated by region yield some of the most interesting results.[31] The study concludes that regional economic expectations of the national economy are an important influence on public opinion, and that expectations are closely linked to objective economic conditions.

Respondents in the north of England, Scotland, and Wales viewed national economic conditions much less favourably than did southern voters. While the study did not disaggregate objective conditions, into, for example, regional unemployment or asset price inflation, the more negative northern interpretation of the national economic situation is natural given the depressed nature of the northern economy relative to the situation in the south during the 1980s.[32] Again, as with the previously discussed expectations model proposed by Johnston, *et al.*, the direction of causality is not clear. The study does not explore whether northern disapproval is more related to partisanship than to the state of the economy.

## CONCLUSION

Several points are apparent from this review. First, the socio-economic model offers a partial explanation for the increased regional polarisation of British electoral results since the 1950s. Changes in the spatial distribution of class and the rise of service workers have altered the electoral geography of Britain. The relationship between class and party explains approximately half of the north–south divide. However, this leaves a large gap still unexplained.

The economic model is also of some use in explaining the north–south divide. Several studies of one or more elections have found that objective economic conditions have some impact on personal expectations and on the vote. However, the relationship is uneven at best and cannot stand alone in explaining regional variation. Short-term economic performance does not explain regional change.

This discussion points to the need for a framework within which to place change and stability. There are institutional structures in Britain separate from class structure and from unemployment and inflation rates; bringing a core–periphery analysis into the voting model may contribute to our understanding of how Britain votes and, more generally, of the external influences that act upon individuals everywhere.

Regional Dynamics

NOTES

NOTES

1. J. Curtice and M. Steed, 'Proportionality and Exaggeration in the British Electoral System', *Electoral Studies*, 5, 3 (December 1986) pp. 209–28.
2. I. McAllister and D.T. Studlar, 'Region and Voting in Britain 1979–87: Territorial Polarisation or Artifact?', *American Journal of Political Science*, 36, 1 (February 1992) pp. 168–99.
3. R. J. Johnston, C.J. Pattie, and J.G. Allsop, *A Nation Dividing? The Electoral Map of Great Britain, 1979–87* (London: Longman, 1988).
4. M. Hechter, *Internal Colonialism: The Celtic Fringe in British National Development 1536–1966* (Berkeley and Los Angeles: University of California Press, 1975); W. L. Miller, *The End of British Politics? Scots and English Political Behaviour in the Seventies* (Oxford: Clarendon Press, 1981); S. Kendrick and D. McCrone, 'Politics in a Cold Climate: The Conservative Decline in Scotland', *Political Studies*, 37, 4 (December 1989) pp. 589–603.
5. D. Butler and D. Stokes (1974), Ch. 6; see also Ch. Two above.
6. D. Butler and D. Stokes, *Political Change in Britain* (London: Macmillan, 1969) pp. 138–43.
7. M. Eagles, 'An Ecological Perspective on Working-Class Political Behaviour', in R.J. Johnston, F. Shelley, and P. Taylor (eds), *Developments in Electoral Geography* (London: Routledge, 1990).
8. C.T. Husbands, *Racial Exclusionism and the City* (London: Allen and Unwin, 1983), Ch. 3.
9. M. Harrop, A. Heath, and S. Openshaw, 'Does Neighbourhood Influence Voting Behaviour – and Why?', in I. Crewe, P. Norris, D. Denver, and D. Broughton (eds), *British Elections and Parties Yearbook: 1991* (London: Harvester Wheatsheaf, 1992).
10. Socio-economic groups 7 (personal service workers), 8 (foremen and supervisors – manual), 9 (skilled manual workers), 10 (semi-skilled manual workers), 11 (unskilled manual workers) and 15 (agricultural workers).
11. A.F. Heath, R. Jowell, J. Curtice, G. Evans, J. Field, and S. Witherspoon, *Understanding Political Change: The British Voter, 1964–1987* (Oxford: Pergamon Press, 1991) p. 203.
12. McAllister and Studlar.
13. Ibid., p. 182. The controls used include parental partisanship, father's occupation, socio-economic status (education, occupation, and unemployment), economic life-style (housing tenure, income, and trade union membership) and ascribed characteristics (age, gender, and race).
14. Ibid., pp. 190–1.
15. C. Pattie, E. Fieldhouse, R. Johnston, and A. Russell, 'A Widening Regional Cleavage in British Voting Behaviour: Some Preliminary Explanations', in I. Crewe, P. Norris, D. Denver, and D. Broughton (eds), *British Elections and Parties Yearbook: 1991* (London: Harvester Wheatsheaf, 1992).
16. T. Brown, *Migration and Politics* (Chapel Hill NC: University of North Carolina Press, 1988).
17. D. Denver and K. Halfacree, 'Inter-Constituency Migration and Party Support in Britain', *Political Studies*, 40, 3 (September 1992) pp. 571–80.
18. D. McMahon, A. Heath, M. Harrop, and J. Curtice, 'The Electoral Consequences of North–South Migration', *British Journal of Political Science*, 22, 4 (October 1992) p. 442.
19. W.H. Field, 'Council Housing and the Expansion of a Conservative Electorate: Some Aggregate Results and Their Causes', paper presented at the Annual Meeting of the Political Studies Association Specialist Group on

Elections, Parties, and Public Opinion, Great Northern Hotel, London, 15–17 September 1995.

20. For a more complete development of economic models of voting, see Chapter One above.

21. Quoted in E. Tufte, *Political Control of the Economy* (Princeton: Princeton University Press, 1978) p. 3.

22. D. A. Irwin, 'The Politics of Free Trade: Voting in the British General Election of 1906', *Journal of Law and Economics* 37, 1 (April 1994), pp. 75–108; D. A. Irwin, 'Industry or Class Cleavages over Trade Policy? Evidence from the British General Election of 1923', National Bureau of Economic Research, Inc., Working Paper No. 5170, 1995.

23. *The Economist* reports that, at the height of the 1990–92 economic downturn, the four daily and four Sunday newspapers of the quality press included stories with the word 'recession' an average of almost 5,000 times each quarter. That comes out to about 55 stories per day spread over the titles, or 13 stories per issue per day on the recession (see *The Economist*, 11 September 1993). The tabloid press also covered the recession widely, as did television news, so it is unlikely that any active member of the British electorate was unaware of the economy at that time.

24. J.R Owens and L.L. Wade, 'Economic Conditions and Constituency Voting in Great Britain', *Political Studies*, 36, 1 (January 1988) pp. 30–51.

25. J. Curtice and M. Steed, 'The Results Analysed', in D. Butler and D. Kavanagh (eds), *The British General Election of 1987* (New York: St. Martin's Press, 1988).

26. Ibid., p. 332.

27. C.A.E. Goodhart and R.J. Bhansali, 'Political Economy', *Political Studies*, 18, 1 (March 1970) pp. 43–106.

28. Johnston, Pattie, and Allsop; R.J. Johnston and C. Pattie, 'Voting in Britain: A Growing North–South Divide?', in J. Lewis and A. Townsend (eds.), *The North–South Divide: Regional Change in Britain in the 1980s* (London: Paul Chapman, 1989).

29. R. J. Dalton, *Citizen Politics in Western Democracies: Public Opinion and Political Parties in the United States, Great Britain, West Germany, and France* (Chatham, NJ: Chatham House, 1988) p. 180.

30. H. Norpoth, *Confidence Regained: Economics, Mrs. Thatcher, and the British Voter* (Ann Arbor: University of Michigan Press, 1992) pp. 62–3.

31. D. Marsh, H. Ward, D. Sanders, and S. Price, 'Modelling Government Popularity in Britain, 1979–87: A Disaggregated Approach', in I. Crewe, P. Norris, D. Denver, and D. Broughton (eds), *British Elections and Parties Yearbook: 1991* (London: Harvester Wheatsheaf, 1992).

32. Ibid., p. 85.

# CHAPTER FOUR

# The Core–Periphery Cleavage: Concepts and Interpretations

CORE–PERIPHERY analysis has been used to examine a wide variety of political phenomena pertaining to the mobilisation of electorates along cleavage lines.[1] At its most basic level, the approach suggests that differences between a country's heartland (the core) and outlying areas (the periphery) contribute to the alienation of some residents from the power structures of the country. The core–periphery cleavage is a condition in which spatially differentiated factors alienate people who are geographically remote from society's mainstream. People in the periphery object to the encroachment of political power, economic forces, or cultural ideas, from the core.[2] The cause of the objection is perceived differences between people in the different parts of the country and the negative effects of the encroaching power on peripheral autonomy. This alienation contributes to the mobilisation of voters into political parties; parties representing a country's core strive to concentrate power in the central state apparatus, while parties of the periphery adopt such goals as decentralised political structures (including devolution), linguistic distinctiveness, or opposition to large corporate institutions.

The utility of the core–periphery construct is well known and has been thoroughly investigated. Research has provided extensive insight into existing regional differences in voting behaviour, ethno-national movements, and inequalities in development.[3] However, in almost all its manifestations, the approach fails to explain *changes* in the salience of regional political parties and demands for devolution. Core–periphery analysis does not explain why a particular political movement gains widespread support at one point in time but not another. This inherently *static* nature in the conceptualisation of core–periphery relations severely limits the usefulness of the concepts for longitudinal explanation.

This chapter outlines a *dynamic* model that gives more explanatory power to the concepts. The static model is measured through the historical development of a particular political system,[4] or through the development of its economic and natural resource structures.[5] In contrast, the dynamic model measures, at the subnational level and at several points in time, a collection of variables that capture the distribution of power across a country. This conceptualisation of core and periphery is based primarily on the social identity of voting that was discussed in Chapter One above, but is also defensible in terms of the economic theory of voting. Individuals join parties of the core or of the periphery on the basis of individual identity relative to larger power structures, and they do so to defend the particular geographic interests with which they identify.

## THE UTILITY OF CORE–PERIPHERY ANALYSIS

The core–periphery approach has advantages in both economic and social identity theories. For the theory of economic voting, it places a long-term institutional framework around the short-term economic impact of such factors as unemployment. In the 1992 general election, for example, the economic condition of Scotland and the north of England was better than the condition of the south-east. As predicted by economic voting, the Conservatives did better there than elsewhere, suffering less relative to Labour in the north than in the south, and actually gaining on Labour in Scotland. Yet at the same time, the Scottish Nationalists increased their share of the Scottish vote by 50 per cent. Such a result is inexplicable unless one understands the forces of nationalism that this analysis provides.

From the structural–institutional, or social identity theory, core–periphery analysis provides an answer to the issue of regional variations in class voting. Often an ahistorical analysis misses the long-standing problems that underlie and guide the progression of a problem such as ethnic conflict. The historical development of economic, political, and social structures contributes to an understanding of contemporary events. To understand such events more fully, an exploration of the regional aspects of the main economic and political events of Britain since the end of the 1981–82 recession is in order. The 11 years of this brief examination provide an example of why London and the Home Counties remain the core of Britain while Scotland remains generally the most distant part of the periphery.

## Britain in the 1980s

During the mid- to late-1980s, the Home Counties boomed. High-paying jobs in financial services in London and the outlying counties increased dramatically. Accompanying this was substantial asset inflation, with house prices increasing in double digits every year for several years. Unemployment vanished as a general social problem. Economic well-being led to a seemingly new ethos among those newly enriched by the Thatcherite version of capitalism – those who became collectively known as 'Essex Man': a faith in entrepreneurial skills, in individual survival, in reward and advancement based on merit, and in the need for the central government to keep local authorities on a close financial rein to limit their exuberant excesses. 'Essex Man' commuted into London, worked hard, and was properly rewarded. In turn, he and his wife re-elected the Conservative government, viewing it correctly as the source of their region's success. In 1987, in the south-east of England (outside London), Labour captured only one seat out of 108 from the Conservatives. Even in Inner London, with all its urban decay, crime, poverty, and working class quarters, Labour won fewer than half the seats that year.

The effects of the 1990–91 recession were still being felt at the time of the 1992 general election. Unlike the previous downturns, this recession struck the south-east much more severely than elsewhere. Unemployment was higher in May 1992 than in June 1987. Business failures, mortgage fore-closures and personal bankruptcies were also higher. In this environment it was widely thought that the Conservatives would do less well than at the previous election. Conversely, Labour was expected at worst to form a coalition government and at best to secure a clear majority by winning more seats in the south-east. In the event, little changed. To be sure, Labour captured 20 of the 29 seats in Inner London. Elsewhere in the south-east outside London, however, while the Conservative vote fell 1.1 per cent, Labour's representation increased to only three seats, and the Conservatives won again with a small national majority. Essex Man, Essex Woman, and their neighbours did not desert the Conservatives; the real electoral battle was between Labour and the Liberals, the latter losing their claim to be the main challengers in the region.

Little changed in Scotland too. In 1987 Scotland was still suffering greatly from the recession that began earlier in the decade. Unemployment was well above the national average, and personal income was well below. By the 1992 election Scottish unemployment had fallen below 1987 levels and below the level in many parts of England. At the same time, anti-London and anti-Tory sentiment was running high, with political devolution at or near the top of all major non-Conservative party agendas. In this climate, economic conditions foretold an improvement in the electoral performance of the Scottish Conservatives while rhetorical conditions predicted a humiliating defeat for the party. In the event, Labour and Liberal Democrat support fell, with the lost votes going primarily to the Nationalists. Conservative support rose 1.7 percentage points while Nationalist support swelled by half, to 21 per cent. Despite improved economic conditions, political support for devolution ballooned. Economic voting may account for the improved Conservative performance but it cannot begin to explain the Nationalist vote. Core–periphery analysis provides this link.

CORE–PERIPHERY MODELS: CURRENT THEORY

The fundamental underlying assumptions about the core–periphery cleavage rest on an unequal distribution of power. Members of one particular area live in close proximity to sources of political, economic, or cultural power, and so align themselves with those who wield a disproportionate degree of influence over the political, economic, and cultural content of a country.[6] Members of outlying regions are geographically more distant from these centres, and so wield much less influence. Inhabitants of the periphery feel a certain alienation as a result of their distance and also as a result of a potential or actual threat against outlying power structures. They can perceive that their economic, political, or cultural prospects suffer from their status. Alienation and limited prospects spawn anti-core political movements.

Despite general theoretical agreement about the nature of the core–periphery cleavage, there are two conflicting sets of economic assumptions that guide the observer's understanding of the past and future of this cleavage in any particular country. These sets of economic assumptions can be differentiated in terms of their theoretical origins: one is essentially liberal, while the other is essentially Marxian.[7]

The neo-liberal model assumes that the periphery is a residual unit that lags behind the core only because of certain accidents of history and geography. The development of an important trading route, or a politico-administrative centre, or a defensible military position, can lead to the creation of a powerful economic and political structure that later spreads its influence further and further afield. When contact with the core begins, the periphery has distinctive cultural traits and more primitive economic structures. Eventually, however, the periphery may be absorbed into the core through the processes of modernisation, industrialisation, communication, and socialisation.[8] Over the long term, members of the periphery will come to accept the same value structures as members of the core, and will share equally in the economic and political benefits of developments. The absorption process involves a long period of domination, however, during which members of the periphery are generally subjugated and then mobilised into anti-core political movements. Political protesters are fighting a senseless, rearguard action against cultural extinction.

An alternative neo-Marxian formulation sees the periphery as an inevitable by-product of economic forces. As in the neo-liberal model, a core area appears through the random accidents of geographic, military, or political history, but the further interaction of core and periphery is not benign. The capitalist, market-based processes of expropriation, capital accumulation, and uneven development inevitably benefit part of the world or part of a country at the expense of another part.[9] A spatial division of labour arises where control over the production process resides in the core while the periphery is limited to producing according to instructions issued elsewhere. Core areas thrive by expropriating resources from their peripheries, while peripheries are destined to remain subservient. The periphery is not a residual area destined for benign absorption into the core; it is an enduring offshoot of the workings of the world economy and a natural extension of a successful core.

Not all countries have developed the same type of core–periphery politics in response to core–periphery structures. In some countries, such as Italy, the lack of convergence between the political core and the economic or cultural cores has led to separatist demands in the economic core. In other countries, such as Great Britain, monocephalic core structures lead to what Michael Hechter called reactive ethnicity as the periphery becomes more, not less, distinct from the core.[10] A third type of country, with a more diffuse distribution of power across arenas and territorial units, of which the best example perhaps is the United States, would show the absence of distinct core–periphery politics. Each situation would be apparent to quantitative core–periphery analysis.

## The limits of the static model: the development of Britain

While both historical analysis and survey research may be very informative, this section discusses more completely the degree to which this type of approach provides an incomplete foundation for understanding the regional politics of Britain.

Core and periphery were in evidence before the most recent rise of Scottish and Welsh nationalism. In the third wave of the British Election Survey, Butler and Stokes found a strong territorial dimension in reported attitudes toward the centralisation of the government in London (see Figure 4.1).[11] People in London and the south-east were quite satisfied with the contemporary level of centralisation, but dissatisfaction rose steadily the further one went from the capital. In the north of England those who were content outnumbered those who thought the government was too centralised by a narrow margin, while in Scotland the malcontents were in a large majority. This distribution of attitudes fits well with a core–periphery pattern at a time when the distribution of partisan support showed less polarisation than at more recent elections.

Evidence of the general stability of the core–periphery cleavage and the hostility to the central government that exists in the periphery can be found in the 1987 British Election Survey, where a similar question to that posed in 1970 was put

FIGURE 4.1
ATTITUDES TOWARDS GOVERNMENT POWER, 1970 AND 1987

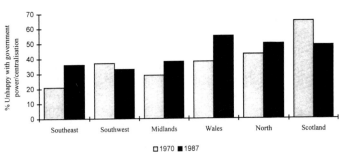

□ 1970 ■ 1987

Source: For 1970, data are from D. Butler and D. Stokes *Political Change in Britain*, 2nd edition (London: Macmillan, 1974) p.139. Bar records the percentage of respondents who thought government was too centralised. Question: 'Some people think that government is too much centralised in London; others are quite content with things as they are. What do you think?'
For 1987, data are from A. Heath, *British Election Study, 1987* (computer file) (Colchester, ESRC Data Archive, 1989). Question: 'And what about the government, does it have too much power or too little power?' Bar records percentage of respondents who thought the government had too much power.

to respondents, namely whether or not the government was too powerful.[12] Attitudes were less favourable in 1987 than in 1970 (57 per cent expressed satisfaction in 1987 as opposed to 64 per cent in 1970) but the same geographical distribution still held: dissatisfaction was higher in the north of England, Wales, and Scotland than in the south.

Attitudes are useful for examining and categorising contemporary societies, but they are not available for Victorian, Edwardian, or Georgian Britain. It would be very useful to have opinion poll results from Victorian England, but this is not possible. In the absence of such survey data, the division of Britain into core and periphery through historical analysis will illustrate the pitfalls of this method.

### Core areas: London and the Home Counties

London is the heart of England and has been since at least the fifteenth century. Commenting on the city's growth in the early seventeenth century, James I remarked that 'Soon London will be all England.'[13] Its attraction for those who desired to make money by trading with other countries, its demand for labour to assist with shipping that trade, and its need for consumer goods to serve the growing wealth of the mercantile and financial classes, led to the most complex occupational structure in Britain, if not Europe, by 1700.[14] This complexity led a commentator to remark in 1681 that

> The bigness and great consumption of London doth not only encourage the breeders of provisions and higglers thirty miles off but even to four score miles. Wherefore I think it will necessarily follow ... that if London should consume as much again country for eighty miles around would have greater employment or else those that are further off would have some of it.[15]

The attraction of the London market and the development of a local core–periphery division of labour are already evident in the trade patterns pictured here.

According to some sources, 75 to 80 per cent of England's overseas trade was handled through London in 1702.[16] Rising wages in London helped spur economic development elsewhere in Britain as retailers sought cheaper sources of labour for the manufacture of their wares in the nineteenth century.[17] Such activity gave the appearance that 'London was, at one and the same time, central yet peripheral, economically secondary yet socially dominant, culturally inspirational yet parasitic',[18] but London's national economic and social importance increased by leaps and bounds.

By the end of the nineteenth century, British industry existed through London's financial, insurance, and mercantilist intermediation. London and its environs had

> a significant though unobtrusive manufacturing base, with consumer-oriented enterprises largely organised in small specialist workshops, and an increasingly wide-ranging service sector, with specialist financial and banking activities centred on the City.[19]

At the same time, the whole south-east was firmly tied into London's network, thanks to the railway system. In 1907, an observer commented that 'in a manner, all south-east England is a single urban community'.[20] Wealthy Londoners had moved out to the suburbs, to previously isolated rural towns in the Home Counties, and had made the seaside resorts along the English Channel their homes-away-from-home. London served its surroundings while the surroundings served London in a tightly knit market which produced its own specialist consumer goods to cater for societal élites. By 1880, 'consumer's England' had arrived.[21] As a political consequence of London's economic importance, the social problems of London became the social problems of the nation: problems of unemployment, poverty, deteriorating housing stock, and crime which plagued London and other cities in varying degree were viewed through the prism of London alone, while solutions were applied equally across Britain.[22]

As the century turned and the transportation network improved, economic power continued to be centred in London and the Home Counties. Today, this area, from the rolling hills of the Channel coast to the fox-hunting countryside around the source of the Thames, monopolises political, cultural, and economic power: the seat of royal government in London and the Anglican Church at Lambeth, the great universities of Oxford and Cambridge, the financial and trading centre of the City, and the richest agricultural land in Britain. The Home Counties are the heart of England.

*Periphery areas: Wales and Scotland*
British history has made Wales an obvious periphery. The political absorption of Wales into England in 1536 did not place the Welsh on a par with their English counterparts; well into the nineteenth century the Welsh were dominated by an English or Anglicised gentry and had little political power of their own. Laws and official discrimination against Nonconformist (Protestant but non-Anglican) church practices, the Welsh language, and Welsh land ownership made the Welsh second-class citizens in their own land. The limited development of education and the hostility of the national government toward Welsh non-Anglican churches did not help matters. The geographical remoteness of most of Wales delayed the growth of industry and inhibited communications networks. Only in the rich coal region of south Wales did the industrial revolution make its mark and here, too, leadership was in the hands of the English. The mountainous topography did not fit well with capitalist production practices, so Welsh agriculture remained predominantly based on subsistence farming. Finally, much political power rested in distant London; the remainder rested with the English and Anglicised gentry.

Wales is territorially distinct from England, and its many Welsh speakers have a group identity based on language. These meet the minimum requirements for politicisation of an ethno-national cleavage.[23] Scotland also has the territorial integrity and group identity to allow politicisation of an ethno-national cleavage; in fact, group identity is even higher in Scotland than Wales, given lower levels of immigration from England and strong local institutions of church and state to bind the Scots together.

None the less, Scotland is slightly more problematic than Wales on a number of other counts. A Scottish education was for a time prized throughout Europe and Scottish thinkers were very important contributors to the development of democracy, capitalism, and industrial technology. Scottish leaders were at the forefront of the advance of the British Empire. Furthermore, the Scottish lowlands were themselves an important industrial centre, as Michael Hechter's *Internal Colonialism* inadvertently shows.[24] Where all of Wales lagged behind England economically, the Scottish lowlands matched or surpassed English achievements throughout most of the early industrial revolution. With separate and recognised educational, religious, and legal structures, and with Scottish landlords who generally pushed Scottish interests, Scotland had many more advantages than Wales.

With the transfer of the Scottish Office from London to Edinburgh in 1939, Edinburgh again became the capital of Scotland. As such, it can be argued that Edinburgh represents the core of Scotland with the Highlands being the Scottish periphery. Every urban area has its hinterland, and northern Scotland is certainly attached to Edinburgh. The Scottish judicial system is also rooted in Edinburgh, so the city has many of the trappings of a core.

None the less, circumstances still point to the peripheralisation of Scotland, including Edinburgh. While the Scots had a little political power over their own affairs they lacked power outside their borders. The same could not be said for the English; the predominantly English Parliament was supreme in Scotland and political power emanated from London. In addition, many Scottish parliamentarians had English origins. The Scottish economy was tied to the English one in an unequal relationship that made the Scots dependent on the English market. As industrial capitalism has developed, Scotland has ceded more and more economic power to English leadership so that very few economic decisions are made in Scotland by Scots today.

Geography divides Scotland from England, helping to create an insular Scottish community with little contact with the economic and political centres of British life in the southeast of England. Outside urban Edinburgh, Scottish cultural distinctiveness has not diminished over time, as Deutsch's social mobilisation and communication theory would have led us to expect. Scotland is a separate and unequal partner in its relations with England. It comes as no surprise, therefore, that an active independence movement won 21 per cent of the vote in the 1992 election.

*Ill-defined areas*

Insular communities, dependent economies, political and religious discrimination, and, above all, cultural separateness have all been present at one time or another in modern Welsh and Scottish history. Most key aspects of the core–periphery cleavage still exist between these nations and England. The divide itself is more complex, however. While many categorisations of core and periphery in Britain place England in the core and relegate the other two nations to the periphery,[25] parts of England itself are locked in an unequal relationship with the south-east.

Differences within England are well described by Hobson's 1910 distinction between 'producer's England' and 'consumer's England'.[26] In 'producer's England', life centered around the tempo of the factory, the mine, and the union. In 'consumer's England', all levels of society organised their lives around the leisured demands of the wealthy. Northern England and the south-west peninsula, containing the counties of Devon and Cornwall, with their inhospitable geography, small-scale agriculture and extractive industries, exhibit considerable differences in their economic and social structures from the south-east of the country, with its rolling hills, temperate winters, and rich soil. Industrial Yorkshire and Lancashire, organised as they are around the production of primary goods (turning iron into steel and cotton and wool into cloth especially), have also been different. These are part of 'producer's England'. A model presented by Michael Steed also places them in the periphery, while Miller's alternative model adds Cheshire to the list.[27]

The Midlands, with the industrialised cities of Birmingham and Coventry, are also part of 'producer's England' and so should probably be placed in the periphery too. The same could be said for East Anglia, where the primary focus of much of daily life has been on the fishing industry. At the same time, the early rise of commercial agriculture at the expense of small-scale farming argues that the Midlands, including East Anglia, should be placed in the core.

The degree of confusion over which particular parts of England belong in the core and which belong in the periphery points to the problem with this static approach. When a debate arises about model specification, the 'best' core–periphery model becomes the one that fits the voting data best. Figure 4.2 portrays core and periphery regions in Britain, and marks areas that could fall into either category according to the whim of the analyst. Much of the central part of the island, with a substantial portion of its population and much of its heavy industry, is not easily defined. Although each model discussed traces the historical development of Britain, the discrepancy between them shows the arbitrary nature of models that try to force the broad sweep of history into precise boundaries.

In the absence of some geographical or historical event (such as the recent eradication of a national boundary), there is no reason to think of core and periphery as separate categories; it makes much more sense to think of them as two ends of a continuum. Thus, geographic areas in Britain can be placed on a core–periphery gradient as the social structure, cultural norms, and economic organisation of their separate societies vary. The conceptualisation of core and periphery as a continuum simplifies the problem of the 'ill-defined' areas. The theorist is no longer required to force ambiguous areas into the core or the periphery; rather, they may be placed between the extremes, near the middle of the continuum.

The introduction of a gradient also allows the possibility that elements of the core may lose some of their 'core-ness' over time while elements in the periphery may become more like the core. Peripheries may also become more peripheral through changes such as the exhaustion of natural resources or the closing of major transportation links. This potential for regional transformation suggests that it could be useful to develop a dynamic model where geographical units are sampled repeatedly over time to develop a changing picture of core and periphery areas.

FIGURE 4.2
CORE AND PERIPHERY: A STATIC MODEL

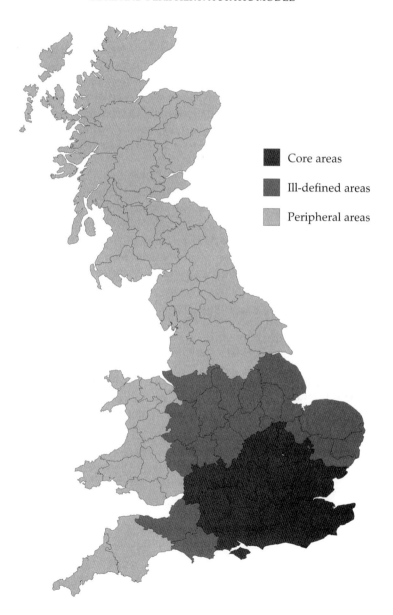

Core areas

Ill-defined areas

Peripheral areas

PARTY LOCATION AND THE CORE–PERIPHERY CLEAVAGE

The development of the dynamic core–periphery model and its relation to voting patterns in Britain follows in the next chapter. The model is used to evaluate the basis of electoral support for the Conservative Party since 1885. Before launching into this, however, it is necessary to discuss the extent to which the parties, especially the Conservative Party, fit a core–periphery model. If there is no reason to suspect that a party has a core–periphery dimension, then there is little justification for providing an explanation based on that dimension. To conclude that voting patterns reflect a division of Britain into core and periphery regions, it is not sufficient to show that Britain is composed of these areas; it is also necessary to place the parties along the core–periphery continuum in a way that is independent of voting patterns. This placement is not difficult.

Britain's three main parties may be clearly and unequivocally defined as representing one side or the other of the core–periphery cleavage. Over the years of this study, their positions on issues vital to the core–periphery divide have not changed through two world wars, a massive depression, and at least one party realignment. The origins of both the Liberals and the Conservatives lie in the cliques that ruled Britain in the eighteenth and early nineteenth centuries. In this sense, both have their roots in the political core. The Conservatives have remained true to their origins, but the Liberals have reoriented themselves as a party of the periphery. Labour, as the party of the working class, was not created to represent either side of the core–periphery cleavage but subsequent developments have led its leaders to position it as a party in the periphery, if not of the periphery. The placement of each of these parties is explained below.

## The Conservative Party

The Conservative Party retained its premodern roots as it developed into a mass party. Describing the importance of religion in the nineteenth century party system, Urwin states that

[t]he marriage between king and church, between local squire and parson, led [the nineteenth century historian Thomas] Macaulay to describe the Church of England as 'the Tory party at prayer'.[28]

After the split in the Liberal Party over Irish Home Rule in 1885, the Conservatives joined in an electoral pact with the Liberal Unionists to champion direct rule of Ireland from Westminster. In the late 1890s the party favoured more intervention in South Africa, winning the so-called 'khaki election' of 1900 on the basis of mobilising support for the Boer War and for the expansion of the British Empire. The early years of the twentieth century saw the Conservatives advocating rearmament to counter the German threat to the Empire. Throughout the period the Conservatives favoured central control of education and bringing all denominational schools into the public sector under a common system of finance.[29] After 1945 the Conservatives chastised the new Labour government for giving up India without a fight and they worked hard (but unsuccessfully) to retain other elements of the dying Empire. Margaret Thatcher even led Britain to war to recapture one of the last parts of Empire in 1982 after Argentina invaded the Falkland Islands. To this day the Conservatives remain the staunchest supporters of a unitary British state, of weak local government dependent on central co-ordination, and of the sovereignty of Westminster. In this context, the admission of the United Kingdom to the European Community in 1974 under a Conservative government remains something of an aberration. The great scepticism shown toward the European Community and now the European Union by Margaret Thatcher and John Major is far more to be expected. Further integration of Britain into the European Union threatens to split the party in much the same way that the Liberals split in 1886 over Irish Home Rule.

Governments since the late 1920s have used Keynesian tools to try to direct economic growth to depressed regions. This progressed most under Labour governments, with major initiatives in the late 1940s and the late 1960s, but the Conservatives have also contributed legislation. In terms of job creation, these policies had been of substantial benefit, creating or saving more than half a million jobs between 1945 and the recessions of the 1970s.[30] Under Margaret Thatcher, however, in the interest of reducing government intervention in the economy, the Conservatives rescinded 50 years of policies focused on reducing the degree of regional imbalance.[31]

Government policy after the end of regional subsidies favoured the core. Tax breaks for home owners, for pension funds, and for London-based conglomerates favoured southern residents over northern ones. A reorganisation of the defence industry and the military had a similar effect. Direct government expenditures in the form of tax breaks and cash benefits aided the richer south by at least six billion pounds (ten billion dollars) more than the north in 1986 – a regional difference of more than five per cent of Britain's total GNP. The Conservative government's policies to cut the highest marginal income tax rate, privatise publicly held corporations, and encourage the sale of council houses to their occupiers also indirectly benefited the more affluent residents in the south disproportionately.[32] That these reforms swayed some voters away from Labour and toward the Conservatives in 1992 makes no difference: Margaret Thatcher saw Britain's problems through the eyes of a member of the wealthy core and her Conservative government promulgated policies that benefited the party's electoral base far more than the truly troubled parts of Britain. The Conservatives began as a party of the core, and remain so to this day.

## The Liberal Party

While the origins of the Liberals lie in eighteenth century élites, the party soon left the path of supporting policies favourable to the existing élite in favour of policies that directly challenged the primacy of core institutions. As the Whigs, Radicals, and Peelites coalesced into the Liberal Party in the middle of the nineteenth century, the organisation underwent a transformation: Nonconformist religious groups took control of the party to further their aim of challenging the hegemony of the Established Anglican Church. Liberal governments overturned laws that recognised only Anglican marriages and they opened Oxford and Cambridge Universities to Nonconformists. Liberals opposed the Boer War, opposed rearming in the face of German militarism (but led Britain into the Great War), and stripped the House of Lords of virtually all of its law-making powers. Finally, in one of their last acts as a governing party, the Liberals allowed Ireland to become independent in 1922 despite vigorous protests from the Conservatives. Since the 1920s, the Liberals have regularly advocated the creation of separate parliaments for Scotland and Wales. Today, the party is more Europhile than the other national parties and is willing to cede considerable sovereignty to multinational organisations while devolving power within Britain down to the local or regional level.

## The Labour Party

Labour has never been a tool of core élites; it was set up by the trade unions in opposition to the capitalist power structure of the industrial élite. It is a party of the disadvantaged and, due to the geographical distribution of industry, it is therefore inadvertently a party of the periphery. Its roots and current strength lie in Wales, Scotland, and the industrial areas of northern England. The peripheral nature of the Labour Party is more circumstantial than the peripheral nature of the Liberal Party, however. Where the spread of Nonconformist versions of the Protestant faith was caused in great part by existing opposition to domination by the English Crown and the Anglican Church, trade unions appeared in response to patterns of industrialisation brought about in turn by variations in economic geography: the location of cheap energy, raw materials, and trade routes. Labour variously backed the Communist International (before 1920), the European Community (in the 1960s), and unilateral nuclear disarmament (in the 1980s). In this context, Labour's nationalisation of major elements of British industry and finance in the 1940s may be seen as an unsuccessful effort to break the hegemony of the core over the periphery and the working class.

It is something of a curious anomaly that the industrial centre of Britain is not in its economic core. Unlike the United States, where industry and finance grew side by side but separate from the political centre, or France, where industry, finance, and the state grew arm-in-arm into what is now an overpowering monocephalic core, the financial centre of London is rather distant from Britain's industrial centres. While Labour has been strong in industrial areas since the 1920s, the party gained a foothold in London only when that city began to suffer the same ills that have plagued nearly all urban areas in Europe and the United States: middle class flight and urban decay. With the exception of its base in the poor boroughs of London, Labour is a party of the periphery.

## Party power and placement on the core–periphery continuum

The success of the Conservative Party as the natural party of government throughout the period under study can be attributed to its connections with the core economy. It might be supposed, however, that when a party of the periphery takes control, this changes the core–periphery dynamic. If the parties of the periphery base their attacks on opposing the establishment, the general view of the establishment – the core – might change when Labour or the Liberals take power. This happens in the United States when an anti-establishment candidate wins the Presidency. In Britain as in the US, the policies adopted are frequently directed toward undermining the status quo, helping the periphery, and reversing the order of haves and have-nots.

The core does not change with the party in power, however. A periphery party may take power and seize the political levers in the core. Such a party may even succeed in redirecting government spending and policies in favour of the periphery rather than the core. This does not change the inherent locational advantage of core regions relative to peripheral ones, though, and does not change regional electoral allegiances in the short or medium term. The freezing hypothesis makes it quite clear how difficult it is for a party to shift its electoral base from one social or regional group to a substantially different one. The Liberal Party used newly mobilised voters to make such a transition in the years before the start of this study: while its predecessor groups were merely loose coalitions of court notables in the seventeenth century, by the time the party emerged as a modern mass organisation in the 1880s it was a party of the periphery in opposition to the powers and privileges of the core religion, core politics, and core privilege.

## SUMMARY

This chapter has explored the dimension of core and periphery in Britain. The static model of the cleavage was seen to be based on subjective interpretations of historical events. In its place a dynamic model that periodically measures the parameters of core and periphery at different points in time has been proposed. This model is expected to augment the utility of previously explored standard predictors of party support.

A political analysis of core and periphery is not useful as an explanation for voting patterns unless the objects of the vote – the parties – can also be defined according to the core–periphery axis independently of the geographic distribution of the cleavage pattern in society. The parties themselves must adopt issue positions that align along the core–periphery axis; otherwise the axis is irrelevant to the electoral sphere.

The political positions of the Conservatives and the Liberals fall clearly on either side of the cleavage. The Conservatives are the party of the Crown while the Liberals stand against the centralisation of power. Labour is more problematic; although it, too, stands against the Conservatives, it has been willing to centralise power to aid the poor against the prerogatives of the capitalist owners. Only recently has Labour adopted policies that favour the periphery, such as regional government for Scotland, Wales and the English regions.

We have seen how geographic polarisation in electoral results has waxed and waned over the years, and how the parties fit into a core–periphery model. We also have the tools for operationalising core and periphery. With the stage now set, it is time to move to electoral politics. Chapter Five operationalises the dynamic model and develops it into an explanation for British electoral history over the past century.

## NOTES

1. Parts of this chapter were presented to the 1995 Annual Meeting of the Northeastern Political Science Association in Newark, New Jersey, November 1995.
2. Useful recent overviews of core–periphery politics can be found in E. S. Wellhofer, 'Models of Core and Periphery Dynamics', *Comparative Political Studies*, 21, 2 (July 1988) pp. 281–307; and E.S. Wellhofer, 'Core and Periphery: Territorial Dimensions in Politics', *Urban Studies*, 26 (1989) pp. 340–55.
3. E.A. Tiryakian and R. Rogowski, *New Nationalisms of the Developed West: Toward Explanation* (Boston: Allen and Unwin, 1985); S. Kuhnle, P. Flora, and D. Urwin, *State Formation, National-Building, and Mass Politics in Europe: The Theory of Stein Rokkan* (Oxford: Oxford University Press, 1996); W.L. Miller, 'The De-Nationalisation of British Politics: The Re-Emergence of the Periphery', *West European Politics*, 6, 4 (October 1983) pp. 103–29.
4. See, for example, S. Rokkan, 'Nation Building, Cleavage Formation, and the Structuring of Mass Politics', in S. Rokkan (ed.), *Citizens, Elections, Parties* (Oslo: Universitetsforlaget, 1970); and M. Steed, 'The Core–Periphery Dimension of British Politics', *Political Geography Quarterly*, 5 (1986), pp. S91–103.
5. M. Hechter, *Internal Colonialism: The Celtic Fringe in British National Development 1536–1966* (Berkeley and Los Angeles: University of California Press, 1975).
6. S.M. Lipset and S. Rokkan, 'Cleavage Structures, Party Systems, and Voter Alignments: An Introduction', in S. M. Lipset and S. Rokkan (eds), *Party Systems and Voter Alignments* (New York: Free Press, 1967).
7. E.S. Wellhofer, 1988.
8. K. Deutsch, *Nationalism and Social Communication* (Cambridge, MA: MIT Press, 1955); K. Deutsch, 'Social Mobilization and Political Development', *American Political Science Review*, 55, 4 (December 1961) pp. 494–513; S.M. Lipset and S. Rokkan, S. Kuhnle, P. Flora, and D. Urwin.
9. A. G. Frank, *Crisis: In the Third World* (New York: Holmes and Meier Publishers, 1981); T. Nairn, *The Break-Up of Britain* (London: NLB, 1977); I. Wallerstein, *Historical Capitalism* (New York: NLB, 1983).
10. M. Hechter, p. 15.
11. D. Butler and D. Stokes, *Political Change in Britain*, 2nd edition (London: Macmillan, 1974) p. 139.
12. Caution must be exercised in comparing the questions, however, as they are not identical. The 1970 question asked specifically about satisfaction concerning the level of centralisation. The 1987 question about whether the government was too powerful has a different emphasis, but it is the closest the BES gets to the centralisation question between 1983 and 1992. Despite the problematic nature of comparing the concepts, the geographic relationship pertains. See A. Heath, *British Election Study, 1987* (computer file) (Colchester: ESRC Data Archive, 1989).

13. Quoted in E.A. Wrigley, 'A Simple Model of London's Importance in Changing English Society and Economy 1650–1750', *Past and Present*, 37 (July 1967) p. 44.
14. Ibid., p. 55.
15. J. Houghton, *A Collection of Letters for the Improvement of Husbandry* (London, 1681). Quoted in E.A. Wrigley, p. 55.
16. P.J. Corfield, *The Impact of English Towns 1700–1800* (Oxford: Oxford University Press, 1982) p. 71; P.L. Garside, 'London and the Home Counties', in F.M.L. Thompson (ed.), *The Cambridge Social History of Britain 1750–1950. Volume 1: Regions and Communities* (Cambridge: Cambridge University Press, 1990) p. 475.
17. M.D. George, *London Life in the Eighteenth Century* (Chicago: Academy Chicago, 1984) p. 198.
18. P.L. Garside, p. 490.
19. Ibid., p. 491.
20. H. J. Mackinder, *Britain and the British Seas*, 2nd edition (London: Heinemann, 1907) p. 258.
21. C. H. Lee, 'Regional Growth and Structural Change in Victorian Britain', *Economic History Review*, 34, 3 (1981) pp. 438–52.
22. P.L. Garside, p. 504.
23. D. Urwin, 'The Price of a Kingdom: Territory, Identity and the Centre–Periphery Dimension in Western Europe', in Y. Mény and V. Wright (eds), *Centre–Periphery Relations in Western Europe* (London: Allen and Unwin, 1985).
24. M. Hechter.
25. Chief among them being M. Hechter and R. Rose, 'From Simple Determinism to Interactive Models of Voting: Britain as an Example', *Comparative Political Studies*, 15, 2 (July 1982) pp. 145–70.
26. J.A. Hobson, 'The General Election: A Sociological Interpretation', *The Sociological Review*, 32 (April 1910) pp. 105–17. See Chapter One above for a more complete discussion.
27. M. Steed; W.L. Miller, *Electoral Dynamics in Britain Since 1918* (London: Macmillan, 1977) pp. 88–92.
28. D. Urwin, p. 227.
29. M. Bentley, *Politics Without Democracy: Perception and Preoccupation in British Government* (London: Fontana, 1984) p. 306.
30. B. Moore, J. Rhodes, and P. Tyler, *The Impact of Regional Policy on Regional Labour Markets* (Cambridge: Department of Applied Economics, Cambridge University, 1981).
31. P. N. Balchin, *Regional Policy in Britain: The North–South Divide* (London: Paul Chapman, 1990) p. 65.
32. Ibid., pp. 78–80.

# CHAPTER FIVE

# A Dynamic Model of Core and Periphery

THE EVIDENCE in Chapter Two suggested that the core–periphery cleavage that affected British politics in the Edwardian era has reappeared in recent years. There is no geographical evidence, however, that a similar cleavage was in effect during the 1950s. A static model, defining the south and Midlands as the core and the rest of Britain as the periphery has little utility in explaining election outcomes between about the 1930s and 1960. This chapter develops the dynamic model introduced in the previous chapter and gauges its utility for describing elections since 1885. For the sake of simplicity, the chapter focuses on the elections where the regional polarisation was at its greatest, in January 1910, and the parliamentary election of 1992. The elections of 1922 and 1955 are also studied as representing periods of minimal regional variation.

## THE UTILITY OF THE DYNAMIC MODEL

The dynamic model of core and periphery serves two distinct functions. The first relates to the more theoretical issue of defining the fundamental elements of the concept. This process of definition is a key part of developing the concepts of core and periphery as robust tools for explaining political change. The second function relates to connecting core and periphery to voting outcomes. Each of these is discussed in turn.

## Core and periphery: robust theoretical tools

By defining core and periphery in terms of variables that measure the concrete distribution of power, the dynamic model strives to operationalise the essence of the core–periphery concept. Once the process of nation-building is complete, the static core–periphery cleavage loses its power to explain change. The force of the cleavage is spent, and its impact becomes mere 'embellishment and detail'. However, a slightly different interpretation allows the concepts to maintain their influence.

Politics, in its crudest sense, is about power and access to power. All cleavages divide people into groups on the basis of characteristics that place them on opposite sides of a particular debate. Thus, for example, the class cleavage involves a debate over who should control the means of production, and the characteristic that generally divides people is whether they are employees or employers, workers or owners. The core–periphery cleavage is also about power, but here people are divided in geographical terms. If power is concentrated in one region of the country, as opposed to in one social class, then opposition to that power structure comes from what is called the periphery. Those who have power, or who are connected to power, are part of the core; those without it are part of the periphery.

A region's place in the power matrix is rarely a black-and-white affair, however; as shown in Chapter Four, many regions are likely to fall somewhere between the powerful and the powerless. It might therefore be better to describe the core–periphery matrix as a continuum, with certain areas being more core-like or peripheral, but most areas somewhere between. Measuring regions in this way allows a region to exhibit some characteristics of a core area and some of a peripheral area without being forced exclusively into either category. With the dynamic model, the core is the core not because of proximity to London or attachment to Roman patterns of government but as a result of connections to political, economic, or cultural power structures.

## Core and periphery: explaining electoral change

The proposed model improves the core–periphery cleavage's ability to explain electoral change in two ways. First, it allows the boundary between core and periphery to vary over time and so regional voting behaviour can be traced in part to changing degrees of proximity to power. For example, when a particular city or county changes from supporting to opposing a party of the core, this can be traced to the elimination of a regional power centre. Counties can move from core to periphery, and vice versa; they are not immutably fixed.

Second, and of greater importance, the salience of the core–periphery cleavage can be allowed to vary: if the periphery becomes more like the core over a period, whether measured in terms of wealth, transportation relations, economic structures or cultural identity, then an explanation for electoral change becomes evident. The construction of new roads to connect a particular part of the periphery to other territories can change the degree of influence residents feel they have over their own lives. This change may be true even if counties in the periphery do not move to join the core; a higher degree of power may change the electoral position of their voters. On the other hand, if differences between core and periphery increase, for example through increased central domination over local government decisions, this may translate into greater regional differentiation in political positions and voting behaviour. By offering a fluid boundary between core and periphery, and by allowing differences between the regions to increase and decrease, a dynamic model offers a new way to examine the impact of the core–periphery continuum on politics.

The static model offers no intrinsic explanation for changing levels of regional differentiation. Studies have shown that regional differences in electoral results can sometimes be explained in terms of distance from London,[1] but that is really no explanation. Why should distance from London have an impact in the 1983 or 1987 election, but not in the 1950 election? Some explanation which the traditional core and periphery model does not address lies behind this phenomenon.

The dynamic model, on the other hand, offers a potential explanation. The boundary between core and periphery and the salience of the core–periphery cleavage can translate logically into electoral consequences. A periphery population that finds itself catching up with the core may have more cause to embrace the parties and policies of the core, while a population that is losing ground would find more reason to object to those parties and policies. In addition, people who find themselves between the 'extreme Center and the extreme Periphery'[2] fit a continuous model better than a dichotomous one.

One of the prime political indicators of a disaffected periphery is the presence of a separatist political movement. In his classic book, *Exit, Voice, and Loyalty*, Hirschman suggested that people who find their life chances negatively affected by their group membership have three choices: leaving the group (exit), complaining about their membership (voice), or doing nothing (loyalty).[3] The most anti-core activity is exit – advocating full independence. Movements favouring independence or devolution existed in Scotland and Wales in the late 1800s and have gained strength again in recent years. This suggests that the salience of the cleavage under discussion receded about the time of the First World War and has re-emerged. However, no movements of any consequence have emerged in peripheral England. This could be due to an error in the geographic space defined as the periphery, or it could be due to sociocultural factors such as the lack of a non-English group identity which limits the development in England of attitudes favouring nationalist movements. An investigation of the distribution of power across Britain can only help to illuminate the actual causes by providing a concrete, structurally based definition of the core–periphery continuum.

A FRAMEWORK

Several technical issues must be considered before choosing which variables to incorporate into the dynamic core–periphery model. These include the questions of sampling the British political economy, of choosing the appropriate unit of analysis, and of taking care to maintain conceptual validity across the years. Following brief discussions of these matters the argument will proceed to the identification of core and periphery through variable selection.

## Sampling

The measurement of any selected criteria can either be carried out on a continuous basis, by measuring every year, or by drawing samples every few years, to capture cumulative change over time. The richest source of data comes from the national census, which is carried out only every ten years. Other data are available even less frequently. This suggests that, from the standpoint of data availability, occasional samples are the best course. To build models that most accurately reflect the socio-economic conditions of the country at any particular time it is important to measure all the criteria chosen at approximately the same time – all within about five years.

Miller's definitive study of voting behaviour between 1918 and 1974 related voting patterns to changes in the class structure as reflected in the censuses of 1921, 1931, 1951, and 1966.[4] He found that changes in the class structure had only a small impact on the geography of the vote and the parameters of regression equations. In essence, any of the four censuses could have been used to estimate the class basis of British politics without substantial changes in the resulting interpretation of the importance of class. For the 1885 to 1910 period, Ken Wald found considerable evidence that class and religion were relatively stable determinants of the vote between 1885 and 1910.[5] These two analyses suggest that the electoral consequences of class and religious change have been quite limited. Furthermore, they offer evidence that it would suffice to sample the core–periphery criteria only a limited number of times over the 107 years covered by this study while still generating a clear picture of the structural changes under investigation here.

If Miller's view of the census information is correct, then a sample every ten years is unnecessary. On the other hand, two samples, one for the period of Liberal–Conservative alignment, and one for the Labour–Conservative period, are too few to allow for change. Four samples provide a good compromise.

One sample at the beginning of the study, from around 1880 to 1890, is needed to cover the late Victorian and Edwardian periods. It would be safe to assume that the Great War would have contributed to as many changes in the socio-economic structure of Britain as it did to the party system. The Great Depression and the Second World War also affected Britain. To reflect these changes, one sample would be needed in the 1920s and another in the 1950s. Finally, as the social transformations and economic crises of the 1970s and 1980s have wrought their influence,[6] a final sample from the late 1980s would present the current human geography of Britain. Given the decennial nature of the census, it makes most sense to draw samples in 1891, 1921, 1951 and 1991.

This sampling procedure provides four benchmarks against which to judge electoral change. It must be noted that this design does not attempt to explain every wiggle of British politics through this core–periphery model. Short-term events all have their impact. These include such factors as leadership changes, incumbency effects, and the rise of ephemeral issues (such as the uneven response among the working class to the miners' strike of 1984, the combination of fatigue and euphoria that led to Labour's victory in 1945, or the war hysteria that surrounded the 1900 election). The general trend, rather than the finer details, can be discerned through the core–periphery analysis.

This division of Britain's electoral history fits the four eras that are generally used for categorising political develop-ments throughout Europe. The first three eras capture the economic and cultural aspects of the pre-war, inter-war, and post-war periods. The last era, the period from 1970, fits with the disruption that many European political economies experienced following the first oil shock, but the transfor-mations wrought by the uneven economic dynamics in the 1980s are of far more interest than the oil shock itself. The chosen years also fit well with the geographic variations in

British elections. The periods 1885 to 1910 and 1959 to 1992 were times of widening regional disparities in party support, while the 1921 to 1955 period saw the near-elimination of those disparities.

## Units of analysis

The unit of analysis for the determination of an area's placement on the core–periphery continuum must necessarily be the county. For most of the evidence presented below, no data have been collected at a level lower than this. While there are some problems with this choice of unit, such as the large size of English counties relative to pre-1974 Welsh and Scottish counties, and the somewhat artificial divisions that county boundaries impose on a territory, the units that are available divide the country adequately for a reasonable distribution of observations along the core–periphery continuum. Counties are themselves averages. Not every part of every county will fall exactly where the calculation of core and periphery would place it. However, core and periphery are large-scale phenomena, not the by-products of small-scale neighbourhood effects. The political nature of core and periphery indicate that it is the mean score for each county that is important: people have different degrees of connectedness, and behave (and vote) accordingly.

By the same token, standard regions are also inappropriate, as being too few to adequately measure changes in the core–periphery continuum. There were a total of between 74 and 79 counties between 1885 and 1974, given the various divisions of Sussex, Suffolk, and Lincolnshire over these years, and 66 counties in the 1975 to 1992 period.

### OPERATIONALISING A DYNAMIC MODEL

Politics as a power struggle covers three broad areas. The struggle for political power is the conflict over precisely who exercises power. This is a contention over inputs: controlling the levers of power. The struggles over economic and cultural power, by contrast, represent disagreements over outputs:

which interests are advanced, and which decisions are made. These three areas – political, economic, and cultural – represent the basic topics of political debate. A core–periphery cleavage divides spatially distinct groups of people in terms of access to these types of power. Along with a fourth area, patterns of regional interaction, these will be the framework around which the dynamic core–periphery cleavage will be built.

A successful dynamic model will include variables that measure the geographic distribution of these kinds of power. Some may be explicit, such as access to a Member of Parliament or the percentage of economic decisions that are made locally as opposed to those made in a distant place. Others may be more implicit, such as the implications that different agricultural practices have on the world outlook in a particular area. The following sections distil a number of variables from the large constellation of possible choices that reflect the distribution of power along the core–periphery continuum. Variables other than the ones chosen here may also work for the model; of the six selected here, four measure different elements of this power matrix while two reflect the ways in which people in different regions interact with each other.

## Economic characteristics

An excellent avenue for exploration would be the variety and use of high technology. Core areas are likely to adopt technological advances faster than periphery areas as a result of closer connections to sources of innovation. However, diversity and the use of more advanced technology are hard to quantify in the industrial arena. Social scientists may be able to differentiate more advanced technology from less advanced technology when they see it, but the historical record is unusually sparse in recording the geographic distribution of the employment of different levels of technology at any particular point in time. One would have to assume that a particular industry used a more or less advanced technology, plot the distribution of that industry based on census reports of employment patterns, and hope that the exercise was conceptually valid over the entire period – a difficult prospect, to say the least.

## Agriculture

The agricultural sector represents a more promising line of inquiry. While time and progress have done much to change the nature and distribution of industrial and service sector employment, it has been a different story for the farmer. Technology has changed the face of agriculture, making economies of scale realisable, reducing employment, and concentrating production as never before. Nevertheless, agricultural practices themselves have changed much less than industrial ones: farming still involves an individual, on foot or mounted, planting and tending seeds or engaging in animal husbandry in manners not entirely different from those used a hundred years ago. The continuities inherent in agriculture lend this mode of production to core–periphery analysis.

From our understanding of the differences between core and periphery, we would expect the periphery to tend more toward subsistence farming or production with lower technological investment relative to the core. Agriculture in the core should take place on a small number of larger farms with higher levels of capital investment. Crop production has become increasingly centralised over the years. Economies of scale have reduced the costs of production on large farms relative to small farms. There has been a centralisation and consolidation of many cattle (especially for milk production) in an ever-shrinking number of farms, with farmers adopting increasingly capital-intensive practices. Farm size and the employment of technology would both be fruitful measures, but data are not readily available over the whole period. A promising alternative is the raising of sheep either for meat or for wool. This mode of farming involves minimal technology, is still practised on a small scale, and has long been common throughout Britain.

The relative importance of agriculture in all modern industrial economies has fallen considerably since the late nineteenth century. Furthermore, wool as a source of material for clothing has also declined as a result of the development of artificial fabrics. The place of sheep in the core–periphery continuum is therefore hardly perfect. Nevertheless, the requirements of sheep farming have not changed: sheep require simple shelter, open space for grazing, and somewhat skilled farmers to raise the animals and shear the wool. Land available for sheep farming is also available for other kinds of agricultural production, and can usually be put to other agricultural uses. The ability to substitute sheep herding with other forms of land use, and the low technology involved, suggest that this is a good measure of production differences and economic power.

Britain today has the largest average farm size, and the most productive farmers, of all the countries in the European Union. However, sheep farming is not as responsive to economies of scale as crop tilling or dairy farming. Since the end of the clearances in the early nineteenth century there has been less room for productivity improvements than elsewhere in the agricultural sector. Unlike land used for crop production, where output can be increased through the application of fertiliser and the introduction of new technologies, land used for sheep grazing is not available for more intensive exploitation. Because the opportunity for substituting higher value-added production is always present, farmers who retain a focus on sheep are, to some extent at least, intentionally remaining outside modern economic power structures. As such, a concentration of sheep farming relative to other types of agriculture represents an area of economic marginality.

Data on agricultural practices have been reported in the Agricultural Returns (published annually since 1866). These data report the number of sheep and cattle on farms in each county of Britain, as well as the total acreage devoted to farming. Data on the relative importance of sheep are derived from these returns. Ideally, this measure should express the importance of sheep husbandry in terms of the market value of wool and meat produced as a percentage of the total value of agricultural output in each county. For a variety of reasons, however, these data are not available. The only comparable data relate to the total acreage devoted to sheep production.

FIGURE 5.1
SHEEP PER ACRE OF AGRICULTURAL LAND BY COUNTY RELATIVE TO
NATIONAL SHEEP POPULATION DENSITY

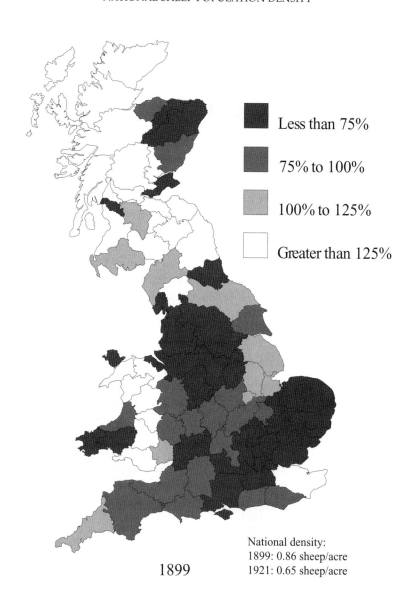

Less than 75%

75% to 100%

100% to 125%

Greater than 125%

National density:
1899: 0.86 sheep/acre
1921: 0.65 sheep/acre

1899

*A Dynamic Model*

FIGURE 5.1 (continued)
SHEEP PER ACRE OF AGRICULTURAL LAND BY COUNTY RELATIVE TO
NATIONAL SHEEP POPULATION DENSITY

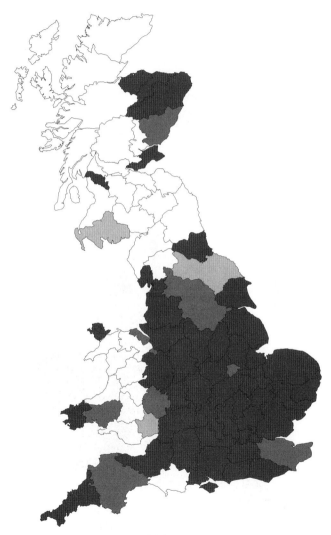

1921

FIGURE 5.1 (continued)
SHEEP PER ACRE OF AGRICULTURAL LAND BY COUNTY RELATIVE TO
NATIONAL SHEEP POPULATION DENSITY

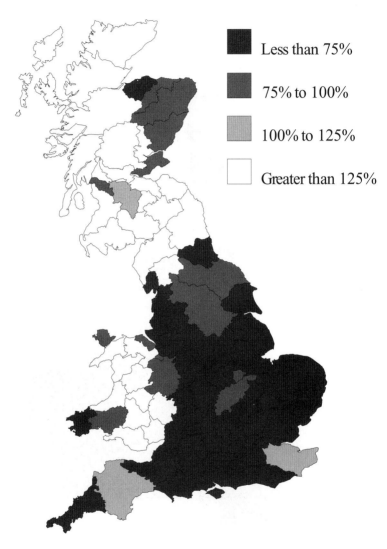

1951

FIGURE 5.1 (continued)
SHEEP PER ACRE OF AGRICULTURAL LAND BY COUNTY RELATIVE TO
NATIONAL SHEEP POPULATION DENSITY

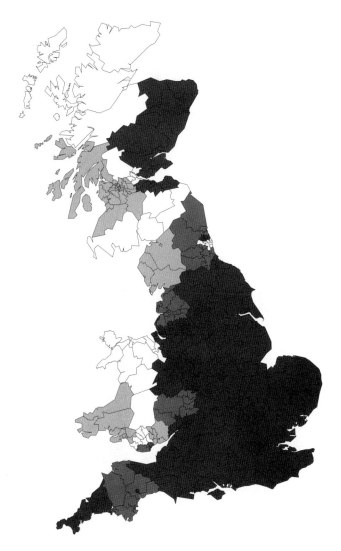

1991

To measure the relative importance of sheep for each county, a figure for sheep-per-acre is calculated by dividing the number of sheep living on each county's farms by the number of acres devoted to farming of any kind. Assuming the land can support the same amount of grazing throughout the country (a heroic assumption that will be re-examined below), this measure will show the relative importance of sheep farming.

A change in the data collection method forces an adjustment in the reported statistics to make the scales comparable over time. The early censuses did not include 'nursery grounds, woods and plantations, or unenclosed mountain and heath land' although the mountainous uplands of England, Wales, and especially Scotland were used extensively for sheep farming.[7] Data for 1991 do include this land in county totals for agricultural holdings. Consequently, whereas in 1899 it appears that the Scottish Highlands had as many as 4.5 sheep per acre (in Inverness), returns from the 1991 census for the same general region report only about two sheep per acre, although the number of sheep in all of Scotland rose from 7.6 million in 1899 to 9.0 million in 1991.

Only six per cent of the almost purely rural county of Inverness was recorded as being in use for agricultural production in 1899. Some of the remaining land would have been completely useless (mountain peaks, small tracts of forest, and, of course, the occasional small town or lake), but most would have been marginally productive, unenclosed and unmeasured sheep pasture. After all, Scotland was almost completely forested in the sixteenth century and it was the enclosure movement that removed the trees to make the space for sheep. For Scotland as a whole, only 25 per cent of the land was used for measured agricultural purposes in 1899. The 1991 census reports that 66 per cent was in use for agriculture (with the remaining third being paved, built up, forested, or covered with water or bare rock). The geography in Scotland has not changed in the intervening century, apart from urban expansion around Glasgow and Edinburgh and limited suburban expansion elsewhere. The apparent difference between the agricultural land in 1899 and 1991 stems from the measurement change which can be reversed by removing 'rough grazing' land (heath, deer forest, unenclosed pasture) from the 1991 agricultural area. This reduces agricultural land by 93 per cent in Inverness, resulting in a total acreage that is far closer to that using the earlier definition. It also makes some correction for variations in the productivity of the land itself: an acre of rich bottom land in the south is far more comparable in productive capacity to an acre of good land in the north than to an acre of upland heath.

One county registered no sheep during the whole period of this study: the territory governed by the London County Council and its successor bodies. Even by 1899 the area had become so urban that no sheep farming survived, or at the very least it was so rare that the authorities made no note of it. The area with the highest sheep concentration is the Scottish Highlands, especially Argyll and Inverness. Between 1899 and 1951 there is general continuity in sheep farming density but enough variation across time and space to suggest a few patterns.

Nationally, there was an average of 0.86 sheep per acre of agricultural land in 1899. In that year, sheep farming played the smallest part of total agricultural production in the Home Counties of Surrey, Middlesex, Hertfordshire, Bedfordshire, and Essex. These counties served as market gardens producing vegetables and such for the burgeoning London population.[8] In fact, sheep farming was relatively unimportant throughout all of southern and central England, excepting Kent, Cornwall, and tiny Rutland, while it dominated agriculture in most of Wales and Scotland, excluding much of north-east Scotland, Fife, and Renfrewshire. This is illustrated in the first map of Figure 5.1, where areas that reported the fewest sheep per acre of agricultural land are shaded the darkest.

The pattern for 1921 is identical except for the Scottish counties of Ross and Cromarty, Lothian, Stirlingshire and Perth, where sheep became less important. Nationally, an average of 0.65 sheep roamed on each acre of farmland. The slight reduction in the importance of sheep farming suggests a minor shift in these areas toward production structures more in the model of the core than the periphery, but the shift is small and is partially reversed in 1951. Interestingly, the Conservative Party won more than half the vote in north-east Scotland in 1951, but not in 1910. While the patterns in Figure 5.1 show only slight changes, there are parallels with election results.

In the period to 1991, 1.96 sheep grazed on each acre of farmland. Areas of above-average concentration on sheep farming include northern England and the western marches, as well as the traditional areas of the Scottish Highlands and the Welsh uplands. The increase in northern England parallels a fall in Conservative fortunes from 40 per cent of the seats in 1951 to 32 per cent in 1992. In north-east Scotland, the relative absence of sheep farming occurs in an area where the Conservatives won a quarter of the seats; by contrast, they won only one-eighth in the Highlands. Again, a slight pattern is apparent: there is an association between a reduced role for sheep farming in what is traditionally known as the periphery and Conservative electoral success. However, the association is weak and insufficient for drawing decisive conclusions.

## Corporate head offices

A second characteristic distinguishing core from periphery considers the degree of economic autonomy or control exercised by production units in a particular place. Cities or counties with many corporate head offices have some local control over their economic destiny, while areas with no head offices for the production units in the area are at the economic mercy of decisions made in distant places. In general, it would be reasonable to assume that head offices would tend to congregate near other head offices and near the centre of economic, political, and social power – namely in the core. The concentration of head offices should, therefore, be an indicator of a core area.

The presence of the head office of a company provides more than just influence or control. The 'head office is not just a building; it is a group of people ... in the administrative structure of the corporation.'[9] Most of these are highly qualified, educated, and ambitious people who are familiar with the workings of political bureaucracies. To a great extent they fall into one or two occupational categories in recent censuses,[10] but census data are not a substitute for the distribution of head offices. The head office is more than a collection of people who work in it; it is a sign of economic competence and capability for the whole city. It is a source of power.

The loss of a head office means the loss of local control.[11] Three problems follow from the absence of local head offices: the absence of local high-level decision making, an uneven geographic distribution of other producer services, and (perhaps) less favourable treatment when decisions about plant expansion or employment reduction must be made. Power is located in the places where important decisions are made and economic power, as expressed by head office locations, is heavily concentrated in the south-east, especially in London. In 1986 only ten of the 100 largest non-financial firms had their head offices outside London and the Home Counties, although 59 per cent of the British population lived outside this area.[12]

The present study is not limited to the top 100 companies, however. The consequences of nationalising the steel and oil industries, coal mining, and the transportation and electricity grids would disproportionately affect the distribution of corporate head offices. Nationalisation led to huge industrial conglomerates with a single head office. Despite this concentration, it is unclear whether the inhabitants of the areas that lost head office staff felt any loss of power. The Conservatives tried to use the local control argument as a weapon against Labour in 1950, but without much success.[13]

Certain criteria were employed in this study to limit the number of corporate head office locations to approximately 1,000 at each period. Any publicly traded company or subsidiary of a publicly traded company qualified for inclusion if it showed a degree of independence by fulfilling minimum capitalisation requirements and satisfied a small number of other criteria.[14] Financial, production, and commercial industries were included while railway and municipal services were excluded in all years. The geographic distribution of head office locations relative to population size are plotted in Figure 5.2 for 1891, 1921, 1951, and 1991.

FIGURE 5.2
CONCENTRATION OF CORPORATE HEAD OFFICES: RATIO OF
PERCENTAGE OF NATIONAL OFFICES IN COUNTY TO PERCENTAGE OF
NATIONAL POPULATION IN COUNTY

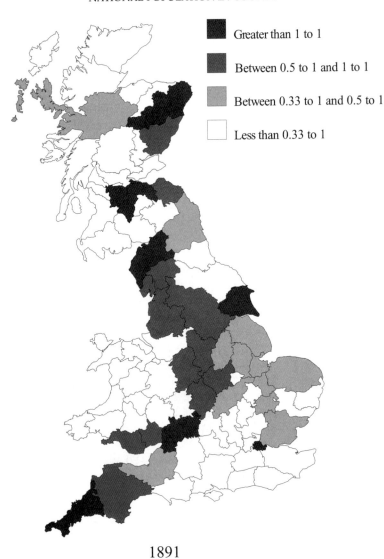

Greater than 1 to 1

Between 0.5 to 1 and 1 to 1

Between 0.33 to 1 and 0.5 to 1

Less than 0.33 to 1

1891

FIGURE 5.2 (continued)
CONCENTRATION OF CORPORATE HEAD OFFICES: RATIO OF
PERCENTAGE OF NATIONAL OFFICES IN COUNTY TO PERCENTAGE OF
NATIONAL POPULATION IN COUNTY

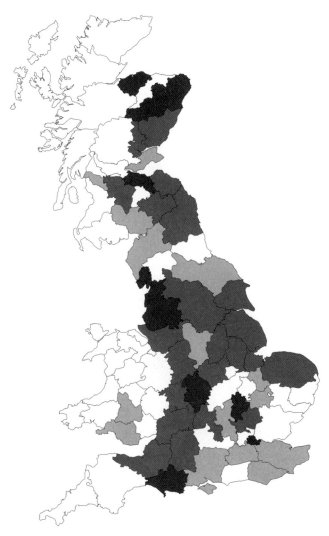

1921

FIGURE 5.2 (continued)
CONCENTRATION OF CORPORATE HEAD OFFICES: RATIO OF
PERCENTAGE OF NATIONAL OFFICES IN COUNTY TO PERCENTAGE OF
NATIONAL POPULATION IN COUNTY

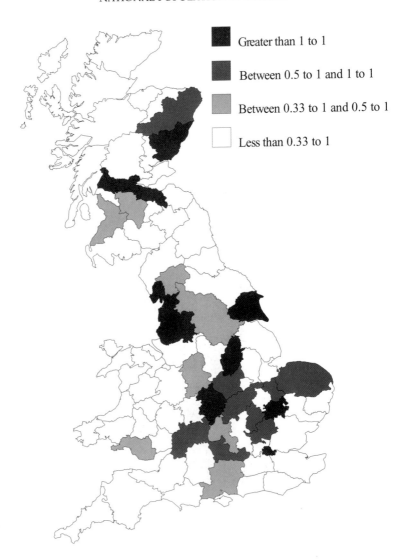

Greater than 1 to 1

Between 0.5 to 1 and 1 to 1

Between 0.33 to 1 and 0.5 to 1

Less than 0.33 to 1

1951

FIGURE 5.2 (continued)
CONCENTRATION OF CORPORATE HEAD OFFICES: RATIO OF
PERCENTAGE OF NATIONAL OFFICES IN COUNTY TO PERCENTAGE OF
NATIONAL POPULATION IN COUNTY

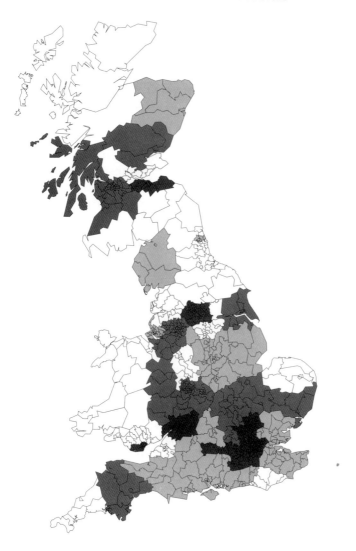

1991

The analysis made no distinction between companies with a single production location and those with many locations. The important issue was the way the locations affected how people perceived their economic independence; while having the headquarters of a large multinational corporation in town is likely to give residents a greater feeling of self-worth than having an independent brewery, both attract the ancillary activities and employment opportunities necessary to the continued self-sufficiency of a town, city, or county. Both provide a degree of connection to the levers of political, social, and economic power.

London's overall pre-eminence throughout the twentieth century is apparent from the maps in Figure 5.2. The local importance of tin mining also appears in Devon and Cornwall, as does the impact of the industrial revolution in the only slightly below- average concentrations of head office locations in the coal mining areas of north-central England. In 1891, London was the most important economic centre in Britain, with 13 per cent of the population but 51 per cent of its head offices. Elsewhere, the only places of above-average corporate head office concentrations were the port cities of Gloucester, Hull, Glasgow, and Aberdeen and the mini-financial centre of Edinburgh. These ports were transfer points for British trade overseas, so it is reasonable to grant them a certain amount of core status in terms of their independence from London.

By 1921, the number of counties where the concentrations of head offices exceeded expectations had expanded to include Bedfordshire in the traditional core, Devon in the south-west periphery, Staffordshire in the Midlands, Lancashire, and Moray/Nairn in northern Scotland. The number of counties where the concentration fell only slightly below expectations also increased, to include most of the Midlands and the Scottish lowlands. The situation was little changed in 1951, with the exception that more of Scotland showed above average concentrations of corporate head offices.

The gains in corporate head office locations outside London had largely evaporated by 1991. In addition to London, only Gloucestershire, West Yorkshire, South Glamorgan, and Edinburgh had above-average concentrations, while northern England and the Scottish lowlands saw their share of head offices fall to below-average levels. The distribution of head offices clearly shows a concentration of economic power in urban areas, most especially in London, at the turn of the century, with that power becoming more widely distributed during the middle years of the century, and becoming concentrated again in recent years.

## Cultural power: newspaper distribution

One important aspect of cultural power is power over news content. In the 1970s and 1980s, the periphery of the world economy – the poorer countries of Asia, Africa, and Latin America – have made persistent demands for increased access to, and control over, media outlets and news content. The assumption behind these demands is that lack of control is one factor that has relegated these countries to the peripheral recipients of cultural goods. Following this logic, a good indicator of cultural power in Britain is the channels of news and entertainment distribution.

Of the many types of news sources available, only one substantial kind has endured since the 1880s: the newspaper. An examination of the structure of newspaper production throughout the period from 1899 to 1991 reveals that there were many more newspapers in London than anywhere else in Britain and that, furthermore, most of the so-called 'provincial' newspapers had London offices. This reflects near-universal agreement among newspaper proprietors that London is the core of Britain.

A standard approach to the analysis of newspapers would be to define London as the core and to compare the distribution of London papers in the provinces to the distribution of provincial papers in London. As well as not being possible, given the dearth of regional circulation data, this violates the basic effort of this analysis, which is to define Britain along the core–periphery continuum without recourse to historical or geographical phenomena – in other words to judge the continuum on the basis of power structures, not on the basis of 'place'. Therefore this measure of cultural power will rely simply on newspaper production, not distribution.

FIGURE 5.3
CONCENTRATION OF NEWSPAPER TITLES: RATIO OF PERCENTAGE OF
TITLES IN COUNTY TO PERCENTAGE OF POPULATION IN COUNTY

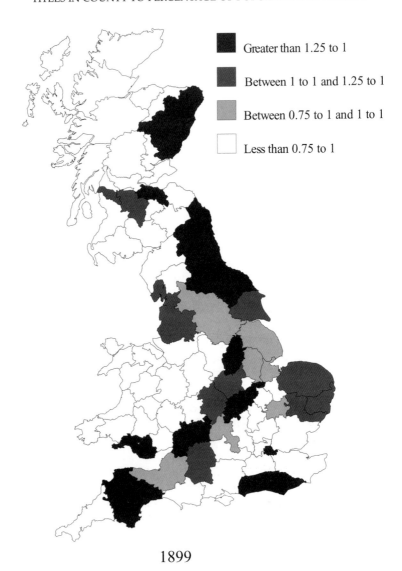

Greater than 1.25 to 1

Between 1 to 1 and 1.25 to 1

Between 0.75 to 1 and 1 to 1

Less than 0.75 to 1

1899

FIGURE 5.3 (continued)
CONCENTRATION OF NEWSPAPER TITLES: RATIO OF PERCENTAGE OF
TITLES IN COUNTY TO PERCENTAGE OF POPULATION IN COUNTY

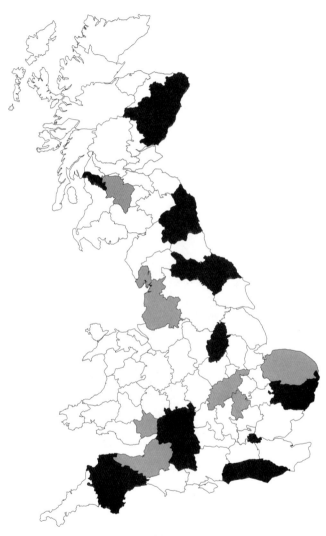

1921

FIGURE 5.3 (continued)
CONCENTRATION OF NEWSPAPER TITLES: RATIO OF PERCENTAGE OF
TITLES IN COUNTY TO PERCENTAGE OF POPULATION IN COUNTY

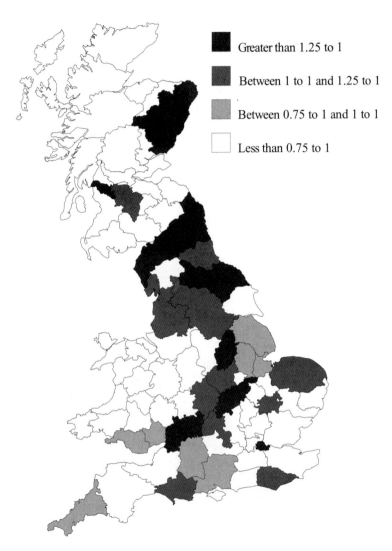

Greater than 1.25 to 1

Between 1 to 1 and 1.25 to 1

Between 0.75 to 1 and 1 to 1

Less than 0.75 to 1

1951

FIGURE 5.3 (continued)
CONCENTRATION OF NEWSPAPER TITLES: RATIO OF PERCENTAGE OF
TITLES IN COUNTY TO PERCENTAGE OF POPULATION IN COUNTY

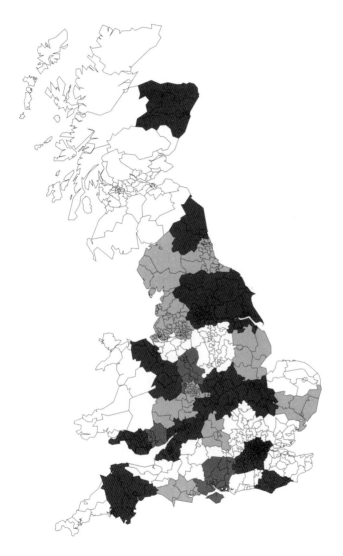

1991

Places that produce more newspaper titles relative to their population are posited to have relatively more cultural power than places that produce fewer or no titles.

Data were collected by county on the number of newspaper dailies published in 1899, 1921, 1951, and 1991. The uneven distribution of population was factored into the data by calculating the number of titles in each county relative to the population of that county. Additional data were gathered on the circulation of the titles in 1991; the correlation between the number of titles and the total circulation by county in 1991 was quite high: 0.79 over 107 titles with a combined circulation of over 27 million. Because circulation data were not available for any but the latest period, cultural power was measured in terms of the number of titles per county at each period.

The maps that comprise Figure 5.3 show a pattern of change that is somewhat similar to the patterns exhibited by the distribution of corporate head offices. In 1899, the earliest year for which data were available, many of the larger urban areas (London, Gloucester, Edinburgh, Cleveland, Newcastle, Cardiff) showed above average concentrations of newspaper titles. These titles undoubtedly served dependent hinterlands but the extent of these hinterlands cannot be measured. By 1921 areas of above-average service had increased, and they increased again in 1951. By contrast with the corporate head office pattern, however, the number of areas with above-average service had increased again by 1991, suggesting the core was expanding throughout the century, rather than contracting again as our initial hypothesis suggested. However, much of the expansion occurred in the traditional core of England: Scotland lost almost all of its over-representation, as did Cumbria, Cleveland, and Durham in northern England. The overall fit is broadly consistent with the expected pattern.

## Political power: élite origins

Just as economic power is concentrated in core areas, so is political power. In systems where legislators are not bound by law to live within the constituencies they represent, the geographic origins of legislators should reflect the core–periphery cleavage. In Britain it is conceivable that a Scotsman would represent a parliamentary constituency in Kent (although it is far more likely for a person from Kent to represent a Scottish constituency). Many English Liberals represented Scottish constituencies at the turn of the century, including Winston Churchill, Herbert Asquith, and Augustine Birrell. Many fewer Scots found political success south of the border.

If there are no geographic limitations on candidate origins, then the core–periphery concept, as it relates to power and control, suggests that MPs would come from core areas more often than from peripheries. Regions that produce more MPs, therefore, could be labelled as being in the core.[15]

Table 5.1 (see page 134 below) shows the geographic origins of MPs for 1892, 1922, and 1951, and of Members who stood for re-election in 1992 and responded to the British Candidate Study. For each part of Britain – the English south-east, the remainder of England, Wales, and Scotland – the table shows a ratio. This ratio compares the share of MPs with origins in each region relative to the proportion of parliamentary seats in the region. A region with a ratio above unity has more Members in Parliament than allocated to it. By contrast, a region with a ratio below unity has fewer Members in Parliament than it has been allocated because individuals from outside the region were elected to represent constituencies within the region. Similar data are presented at the county level in Figure 5.4. When examining this table, it must be noted that the birthplaces of between ten and 30 per cent of Members of Parliament could not be determined. It is assumed that the geographic distribution of the origins of these Members is similar to the origins of those in the table.

The distribution of MPs' origins varies considerably across the years. In 1892 more MPs' had origins in south-eastern England than its parliamentary representation allotted. The English Home Counties and Midlands were in a sense over-represented. Scottish representation was about average, but Wales, northern England, and Devon/Cornwall were badly under-represented. In terms of regional representation, the south-east made up the core, while Wales and the remainder of England fell into the periphery.

FIGURE 5.4
CONCENTRATION OF POLITICAL ÉLITES: RATIO OF PERCENTAGE OF
MPs WITH ORIGINS IN COUNTY TO POPULATION IN COUNTY

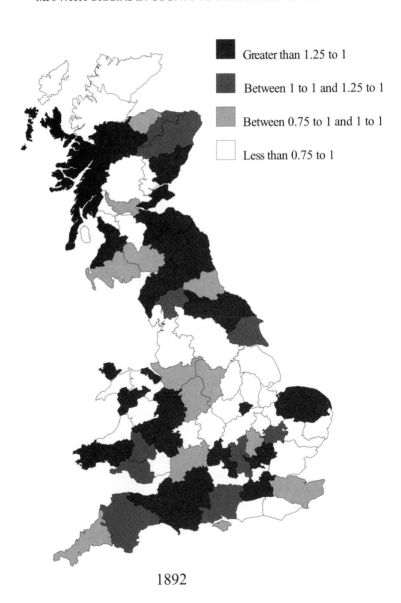

Greater than 1.25 to 1

Between 1 to 1 and 1.25 to 1

Between 0.75 to 1 and 1 to 1

Less than 0.75 to 1

1892

FIGURE 5.4 (continued)
CONCENTRATION OF POLITICAL ÉLITES: RATIO OF PERCENTAGE OF
MPs WITH ORIGINS IN COUNTY TO POPULATION IN COUNTY

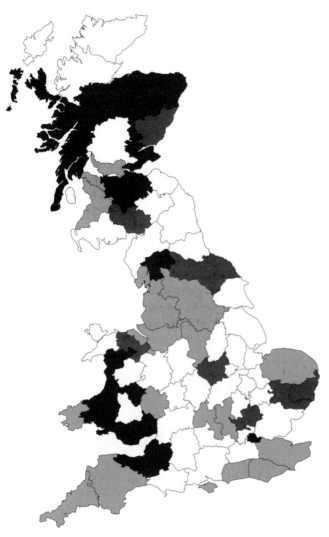

1922

FIGURE 5.4 (continued)
CONCENTRATION OF POLITICAL ÉLITES: RATIO OF PERCENTAGE OF
MPs WITH ORIGINS IN COUNTY TO POPULATION IN COUNTY

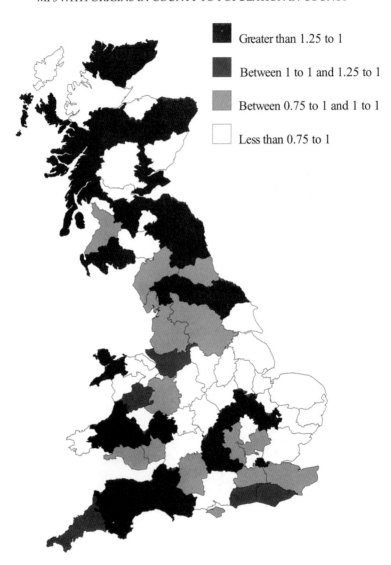

Greater than 1.25 to 1

Between 1 to 1 and 1.25 to 1

Between 0.75 to 1 and 1 to 1

Less than 0.75 to 1

1951

FIGURE 5.4 (continued)
CONCENTRATION OF POLITICAL ÉLITES: RATIO OF PERCENTAGE OF
MPs WITH ORIGINS IN COUNTY TO POPULATION IN COUNTY

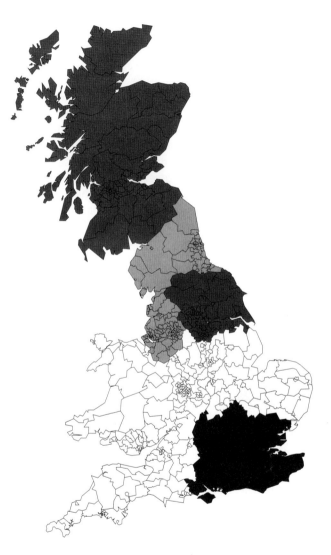

1991

By 1922, with the emergence of Labour as a viable opposition party, the pattern had changed substantially. Northern England remained under-represented. However, while research could uncover the geographic origins of only 27 Welsh Members of Parliament, 33 MPs (five representing English or Scottish seats) could claim Welsh birthplaces. In a similar vein, while 71 individuals represented Scottish constituencies in the Parliament of 1922, and research found the origins of 56 of these, a total of 64 individuals traced their roots to Scotland. The over-representation of Scotland and Wales relative to population increased in 1951, but this is probably more a result of a decline in the population of these areas than to an increased representation from these parts of Britain, given that the under-representation of England did not decline. Nevertheless, the pattern remains clear: the political expression of the English south-east as the core of Britain in 1892 declined until the middle of the twentieth century. A relative change in the core–periphery continuum is apparent.

TABLE 5.1
GEOGRAPHIC ORIGINS OF MEMBERS OF THE HOUSE OF COMMONS IN
GREAT BRITAIN

Ratio of MPs to Seats

|  | 1892 | 1922 | 1951 | 1992 |
|---|---|---|---|---|
| England: South and Midlands | 1.09 | 0.96 | 0.96 | 1.03 |
| England: North, Devon, Cornwall | 0.81 | 0.82 | 0.82 | 0.89 |
| Wales | 0.83 | 1.19 | 1.70 | 0.63 |
| Scotland | 0.98 | 1.14 | 1.31 | 1.03 |
| Total MPs | 569 | 603 | 613 | 576† |
| MPs born elsewhere | 25 | 36 | 25 | 8 |
| % MP origins located | 89 | 79 | 71 | 41 |

† Number of MPs standing for re-election.
Source: See Appendix.

Data from the British Candidate Study[16] are used for the 1992 distribution of MPs who were standing for re-election. The survey did not reveal county origins of sitting Members of

Parliament; data are coded in response to a question asking in which standard region the individual lived at age 14. The regional distribution of these origins shows a reversion to pre-war patterns. The south and Midlands again produced more than the expected number of Members of Parliament, while northern England and the south-west (the English periphery) produced fewer. The over-representation of Wales that characterised 1922 and 1951 disappeared, to be replaced by an under-representation more extreme even than in 1892. Finally, there were more Scottish Members of Parliament than expected given the number of strictly Scottish seats, but not as many more as in the middle years of the century. Again, a relative change in the core–periphery continuum is apparent. These patterns are summarised at the county level in Figure 5.4.

## Interaction patterns

The distribution of political, economic, and cultural power is an important component of the core–periphery continuum. How the regions interact is equally important. Production and exchange relations are a key feature of core–periphery interactions. Data on the regional distribution of industrial production are woefully inadequate for any period in the nineteenth and early twentieth centuries, however, and a similar gap exists for value added and the size and direction of internal trade. While the distribution of geological deposits of primary goods (coal, iron, and the like) is apparent to all but the most casual observer, no data show the value added to that production, much less its regional distribution, in a consistent way. The British collected considerable data on imports to and exports from their possessions, with information on the weight and value of goods shipped to and from each port. Presumably, they had data on the regional distribution of industrial production, from which they compiled national accounts, but they published none of it until the Central Statistical Office was established in 1949. As a consequence, this area of production and exchange is something of a black hole. Surrogate data using the occupational and industrial profile of each county have been used to simulate exchange relations and the spatial location of major sectors of the economy that engage in trade,[17] but these

FIGURE 5.5
POPULATION MIGRATION, RELATIVE TO NATIONAL GAIN/LOSS

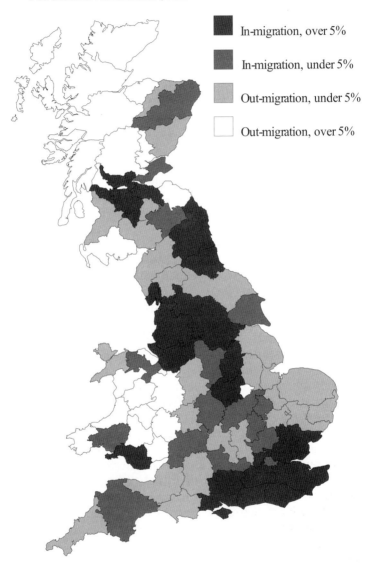

In-migration, over 5%

In-migration, under 5%

Out-migration, under 5%

Out-migration, over 5%

1891

FIGURE 5.5 (continued)
POPULATION MIGRATION, RELATIVE TO NATIONAL GAIN/LOSS

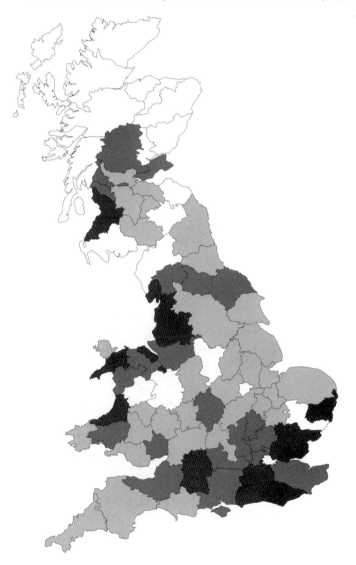

1921

FIGURE 5.5 (continued)
POPULATION MIGRATION, RELATIVE TO NATIONAL GAIN/LOSS

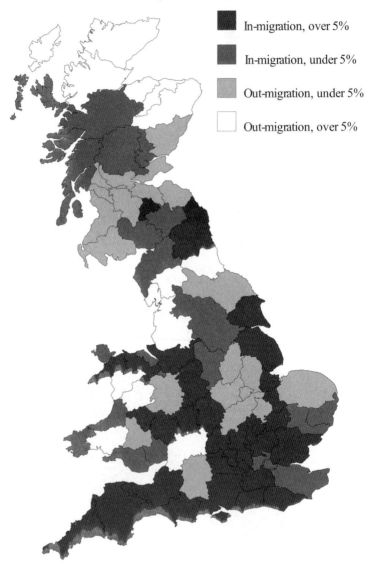

In-migration, over 5%

In-migration, under 5%

Out-migration, under 5%

Out-migration, over 5%

1951

FIGURE 5.5 (continued)
POPULATION MIGRATION, RELATIVE TO NATIONAL GAIN/LOSS

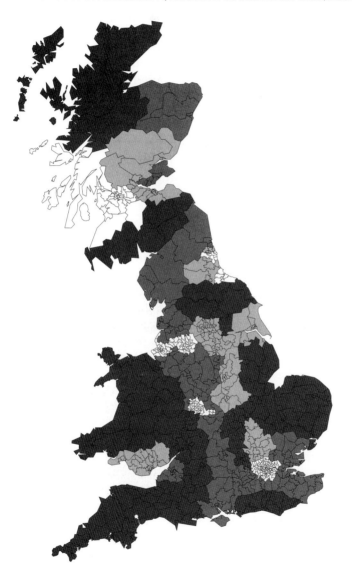

1991

say very little about internal trade and the relative value of that exchange.

Population growth is an imperfect substitute measure. On the assumption that people move toward jobs and that those jobs are generally to be found in the dynamic economic conditions of the core, tracking relative population movement should be a valuable tool for defining core and periphery given the paucity of other data. London's growth from seven per cent of Britain's population in 1650 to 11 per cent in 1750 despite having a higher mortality rate than birth rate[18] is a direct result of its core position in the British political economy. Migration represents a better measure of economic success than aggregate population growth, although it is one that is still seriously flawed.

## Migration

It is reasonable to suppose that parts of Britain where the economy is healthy, robust, and diverse should attract people from those areas where the economy is stagnating or in decline. A vibrant economy needs more workers. If the natural expansion of the local population cannot satisfy that demand, wages increase, and this fosters migration into the area. Alternatively, if a stagnating economy cannot provide jobs for its resident workers, surplus labour is encouraged to move to greener pastures. Even if the economy of the core is not vibrant, its reputation for higher living standards will attract some of those migrating workers. In either case, one would expect population growth in core areas to exceed growth in the periphery in direct relation to the relative economic performance of the two regions.

The data must be treated with caution, however, as the nature of population migration has changed over the years. London has long attracted migrants, being in the early nineteenth century the first and, for many years, the only European conurbation whose population exceeded one million people.[19] Detailed studies of migration patterns suggest, however, that population movement within Britain in the late nineteenth century was marked by 'short-distance movements from villages and lesser towns in the immediate hinterland of the larger, reception, towns.'[20] This initial period contrasts greatly with later mobility patterns.

With the advent of the railway, population migration became easier. It first became possible for people to commute short distances (ten to 20 miles). Inner London began to lose population to new commuter suburbs by the 1890s, and other large cities faced similar problems in the 1920s. As workers began to travel several miles each day, work and home no longer fell so completely within a county.

The decade leading up to 1991 saw an abrupt change in the nature of population migration. Earlier decades witnessed an urbanisation of the British population and a general shift toward the south-east. In more recent years, once-rural towns in Oxfordshire, Berkshire, Buckinghamshire, Essex, and Sussex have filled with London commuters, while the New Town of Milton Keynes has seen its population grow so rapidly that, contrary to usual practice, the Boundary Commission of England promulgated a mini-boundary change to create an additional constituency in time for the 1992 election. During the 1980s, white-collar workers became increasingly prepared to commute for up to two hours each way. Some commuters now drive to London daily from as far as North Yorkshire, while similar commuter patterns exist around other large cities, especially Glasgow.

The abrupt change in the nature of population shift coupled with expanding commuter ranges point to the utility of combining the expanding areas around London with the declining urban core.[21] The inclusion of the migration variable accomplishes this without the need to physically combine different counties: although such areas as Cornwall may fall into the periphery because of the lack of a good transportation network or a low number of corporate head offices, the influx of London commuters would make its *voters* behave more like voters in the core. Migration offsets, to some extent, the measure of corporate head offices in that it includes an indirect measure of the number of commuters. London commuters are more connected to the national economy than the farmers, shopkeepers, construction workers, and manufacturing employees whose prior presence made their rural houses possible.

Each census has tracked the number of people who have

moved into and out of each county in the preceding ten years.[22] British population loss due to migration to other countries amounted to 2.4 per cent of the population in the ten years to 1891, and 3.1 per cent in the ten years to 1921, while migration increased the population by 2.4 per cent in the 20 years to 1951. Between 1981 and 1991 net migration cost Britain as a whole 1.8 per cent of its population.[23] The maps that comprise Figure 5.5 show county-level migration relative to the national level of in- or out-migration over the preceding period. Thus, for example, counties with the darkest shading in 1891 experienced a population increase of –2.4 plus 5, or of at least 2.6 per cent. Counties shaded slightly more lightly experienced migration of between –2.4 and positive 3.4 per cent. The same pattern holds for the more lightly shaded counties and for subsequent years as well.

Rural Wales and the Scottish Highlands experienced the greatest loss of population in the decade preceding 1891, while the counties immediately surrounding London, along with the industrial counties of England, Wales, and Scotland, experienced the highest rates of population growth. On this definition, the most attractive regions in Britain were southeast England, West Yorkshire/Lancashire, Glamorgan, Durham/Northumberland, and the Scottish industrial belt. A tendency to vote Conservative, tempered, of course, by religious and class affiliations, would be expected.

In the decade prior to 1921, London began to lose population to its suburbs; the attractiveness of much of the rest of industrial Britain declined as well. North Yorkshire, Cumberland, parts of rural Wales, and the Scottish lowlands showed the greatest attraction, and would be expected to show higher than expected support for the Conservative Party at the subsequent elections. This trend held for 1951 as well, but the increase in suburban and ex-urban population growth is already apparent by this year, and becomes even more so in the decade to 1991.

## Transportation networks

The final area of investigation concerns patterns of interaction. It is well-recognised that relations between core and periphery are feudal in nature: peripheries only interact with the rest of the world and with other peripheries attached to the same core through that core. The nature of this interaction may best be seen through the transportation network. Transportation in the core serves the needs of the residents: carrying them to and from work and moving goods to markets. In the periphery, however, transportation networks exist primarily to serve the needs of the core and are built to carry goods to core markets.[24]

A difficulty arises which was partly discussed above in the context of maintaining concept consistency: while canal boats and coastal shipping were the primary means of transport in the early nineteenth century, both had been supplanted by the starting date of this study period, first by the railways, and then by the motor car and goods lorry. While the analysis does not need to take into account the growth and decline of the canal, the rise of railways and their decline in the face of rubber tyres and paved roads does pose a hurdle. Furthermore, at the present time road and rail carry different types of goods. Railways are best for carrying large quantities of bulk goods like coal and iron ore for great distances, while lorries are best for specialised shipments of smaller production lots. Measuring one while ignoring the other at any particular point in time would be problematic.

To complicate matters further, no data exist at the county level for railway goods use. Britain is divided into six regions for the annual Rail Returns (published by order of Parliament since the late 1800s) and these Rail Returns do track the value and types of goods and the number of people carried. However, using these six regions would severely reduce the scope for varying the boundary between core and periphery, limiting the utility of the model.

A focus on the transportation of people avoids these problems. The communication model of development[25] suggests that increased interaction can lead to the integration of several small disparate groups into one group with an

FIGURE 5.6
RAILWAY SERVICE: STATIONS PER SQUARE MILE RELATIVE TO
NATIONAL DENSITY

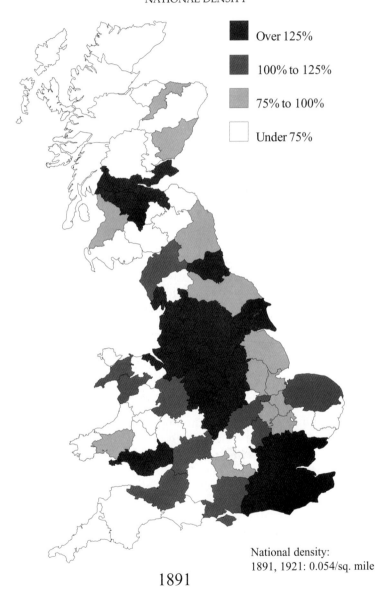

Over 125%

100% to 125%

75% to 100%

Under 75%

National density:
1891, 1921: 0.054/sq. mile

1891

FIGURE 5.6 (continued)
RAILWAY SERVICE: STATIONS PER SQUARE MILE RELATIVE TO
NATIONAL DENSITY

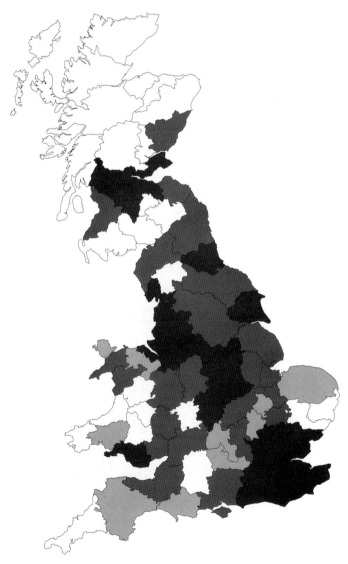

1921

FIGURE 5.6 (continued)
RAILWAY SERVICE: STATIONS PER SQUARE MILE RELATIVE TO
NATIONAL DENSITY

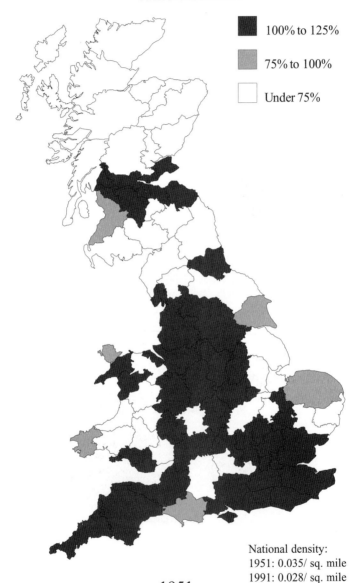

100% to 125%

75% to 100%

Under 75%

National density:
1951: 0.035/ sq. mile
1991: 0.028/ sq. mile

1951

FIGURE 5.6 (continued)
RAILWAY SERVICE: STATIONS PER SQUARE MILE RELATIVE TO
NATIONAL DENSITY

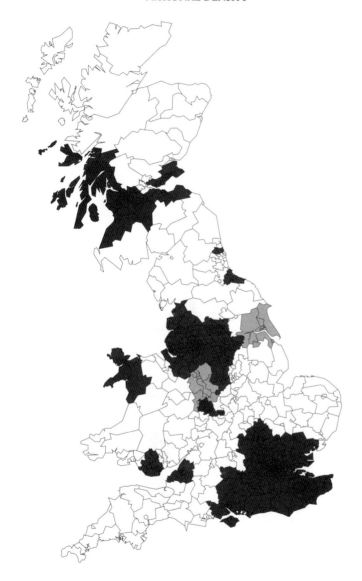

1991

overarching identity. Of course, the opposite is also possible: interaction can create greater differentiation.[26] Nevertheless, the quality of the transportation grid shows the *degree* of contact that is possible between individuals in different areas, if not the *nature* of that contact. Studies of ethnic interactions suggest that the lack of transport and communication networks indicate peripheral areas.[27] The transportation network, therefore, provides an indicator of core and periphery. During the period under consideration, transportation took one of four forms: cart/carriage, motor car, train, or aircraft. Of these, the aircraft is a modern invention unsuited to this historical analysis (although the placement of Britain's two major airports in suburban London supports the view of the area as the core of Britain). The motor car as a popular means of transportation dates from the 1920s at the earliest, so again is unsuited. Trains have been in decline since the 1930s, and some lines have been closed or reduced in scope, but in no case has a previously popular train route been completely replaced by a major road connection. The growth of the motorways has closely paralleled the rail system. The similarity of the networks permits this study to focus on railways as a suitable measure for communication penetration.

## Railways

There are no historical county-level data on the number of passengers carried by trains, their origin, or their destinations. A surrogate is needed. By counting the number of passenger stations in each county, an approximate measure of the level of service in each area can be developed. The source maps do not show the size of each station nor its level of use in terms of the numbers of trains arriving or departing each day, nor do they capture the ratio of long-distance travel to short commuter travel, but a crude count of stations per county does give a rough measure of coverage. In the days before cars, when people were willing to walk, say three miles, to reach the train, an area would be well covered if everyone could reach a station with a walk of less than three miles. Excellent coverage would involve shorter walks, while poor coverage would entail longer walks. Core and periphery areas would reflect this quality of coverage.

Since the arrival of the car and the eclipse of the railway as the primary mode of passenger travel, the British government has been closing stations. There are fewer trains, and fewer stations, today than 75 years ago, but the general layout of the rail network has not changed radically. Stations have disappeared in places where demand was lowest.

Counting stations avoids the problem of high service due to the presence of extractive industries and the need to transport coal and other minerals to seaports and the like. The first trains were built to carry coal and tin from mine to ship or smelter. Before the development of trains as a means of moving people, the British rail network was most developed in the periphery, especially around the collieries of Newcastle and south Wales. Even a map of the rail network in the 1950s shows these coal-producing regions to be as well served as inner London in terms of density of track, but not in terms of stations. People need stations; coal does not. Using the station measure surmounts the problem of a single indicator reflecting many concepts.

The situation in 1891 was noteworthy: while the national railway station density was 0.05 per square mile, density in London was greater than one per square mile and in Middlesex 0.5 per square mile. Assuming an even distribution of stations around the capital, no potential passenger was ever more than half a mile from the train in London. Relatively high concentrations of stations in Surrey, Lancashire, Kent, Glamorgan, and around Edinburgh and Glasgow meant few passengers had to walk more than two miles to meet the train. The rest of industrial Britain was reasonably well served, and poor service was limited to rural Scotland and Wales, and to a string of English counties in the south-west.

By 1921, rail service was better in Lancashire and the Scottish industrial belt (Edinburgh to Glasgow) than in London's neighbouring counties. Overall, the national density was the same as in 1891: 0.05 stations per square mile, but the differences in service between the heavily populated urban areas and the less populated rural counties diminished, and the degree of access became more equal in the following decades. Between 1921 and 1951, a net 700 stations were closed, and a further net 1,600 were closed between 1951 and 1991. Access levels declined as a result of these closures, with much of the East Midlands being reduced to service levels comparable to those in rural lowland Scotland, but the train actually became more accessible in the peripheral counties of Devon and Cornwall.

Access levels in 1991 were fairly poor, with most counties having fewer than one station every 25 square miles. The exceptions were the large urban areas, with their urban rail systems, and the counties that send large numbers of commuters into London every day. The degree to which Kent, Surrey, Essex, Hertfordshire, and Berkshire are tied to London is apparent from the 1991 map in Figure 5.6. Reductions in service elsewhere are also apparent.

The distribution of railway access points began with a concentration of stations in urban areas, the Home Counties, and the Midlands; in 1891 the core–periphery cleavage was somewhat uneven, but still apparent. In keeping with the hypotheses raised in Chapter One, the expansion of the network into 1921 and its subsequent reduction to 1951 reflected a diminution of the core–periphery divide into the middle years of this century. Finally, the years to 1991 showed a more salient divide, and suggest that Britain's transportation structure has returned to the spatial polarisation that characterised the first years of this study.

## Regional change: a summary

None of these six indicators of core–periphery differentiation is adequate in itself for defining Britain's socio-politico-economic space. Each has anomalies or inconsistencies where, because of an inopportune boundary, a particular county appears more peripheral or core-like than an observer might expect. Cornwall appears to join the core on the basis of head offices in 1891, but this is due to the number of slightly solvent, publicly traded mining companies that disappeared over the following few years, rather than to a hidden font of exported culture, a high-quality transportation grid, or an over-endowment of successful politicians. The data must be combined and averaged to create an adequate understanding of temporal variation in the core–periphery continuum. Before proceeding to this mathematical combination let us consider patterns across the variables and time periods.

The only county that uniformly scores as most 'core-like' in 1891 is, not surprisingly, London. Other English urban areas generally score highly as well, with Scottish and Welsh urban areas reflecting these attributes less frequently. With the exception of migration patterns, however, not one other urban area ever approaches London in containing core attributes. Elsewhere, Kent, Surrey, and Sussex reflect these core attributes most consistently. Rural Wales, Scotland, and northern England are least apt to show signs of belonging in the core. While there is unexpected variability, such as the low values for the Home Counties in newspaper titles and head office locations, the general visual conclusion for this sample period is that areas that have traditionally been defined as the core – southern England and the Midlands – are indeed the core on these measures. The uplands of Scotland and Wales, and northern England are clearly in the periphery, while Glamorgan and the Scottish urban belt lie somewhere between the two.

Head offices, newspaper titles and railway stations are somewhat more evenly distributed in the second sample period, 1921. At the same time, migration patterns suggest a weakening in the degree to which the Midlands achieves core status, and more Members of Parliament came from Wales and Scotland than in 1891. While the Scottish Highlands still indicate peripheral status quite clearly, it is more difficult to unequivocally identify the status of other parts of Britain outside the Home Counties.

Migration patterns, sheep density, and the rail network suggest a resurgence of the south-east of England as the core in 1951. The geographic origins of Members of Parliament contradict this, however, as Scotland, especially the Highlands, shows a far larger share of the political élite than expected. The distribution of head offices is also not consistent with a resurgence of the south-east. Once again, as in 1921, the core–periphery cleavage is blurred.

The 1991 distribution of these variables is less equivocal: south-east England is clearly marked as the core in terms of head offices, rail service, élite origins, and sheep. Sheep dominate Scottish farming outside Grampian and Fife, while the preponderance of Scotland is ill-served in terms of newspaper selection and rail access. Wales, too, falls fairly clearly into the periphery on most of these measures. Migration patterns are less clear but much of the confusion in the picture results from the hollowing out of Britain's urban areas in favour of suburban and exurban living. Only the distribution of newspaper titles suggests that the core–periphery continuum runs in any way other than south-east to north-west.

Visual examination of the data provides substantial support for the hypothesis broached in the first chapter that core–periphery politics and the north–south divide closely parallel changes in Britain's socio-political economy. In the late nineteenth century, when London and the south-east dominated British culture and the economy, election results showed an expanding north–south polarisation between Liberal and Conservative (Unionist) support. Between the wars, and in the immediate post-war period, regional differences were more muted both in terms of the core–periphery cleavage and in terms of election results. In recent years, a re-emergence of the periphery has occurred, again in both a socio-economic and an electoral sense.

## DEVELOPING THE DYNAMIC MODEL

The evidence suggests that a core–periphery cleavage polarised Britain in 1891 and 1991, but not in 1921 or 1951. In this section, multiple linear regression will be used to associate electoral support for the Conservative (Conservative and Unionist in 1910) Party to the core–periphery matrix. To do this, it is necessary to combine the six variables that have been chosen to represent the core–periphery continuum into one or more variables that can be entered into the equation.

Of the six variables under discussion, five measure the extent to which the area conforms to the ideal of the core: the more passenger railway stations per square mile, headquarters locations, MPs' origins, or newspaper titles published in the county, or the greater the rate of in-migration, the more the county lies in the core. The last variable, sheep, increases as the county becomes more and more like the peripheral ideal. The standard method of aggregating different variables such as these into a supervariable involves exploring the extent to which they measure similar phenomena through factor analysis and combining the standardised scores of the individual variables. Standardised scores (z-scores) convert the variables into a common scale.[28]

To construct a core–periphery supervariable for the continuum, factor analysis suggests that the variables can be combined into one factor for the 1891 model where the standardised value of the sheep variable is subtracted from the standardised values for the other variables. For the other models, an examination of the eigenvalues suggests that a two-factor model is appropriate. All six variables are combined into one supervariable measuring core–periphery status for 1891, while the variables are combined into two variables for later years.

The two factors could be called 'connectedness' and 'marginalisation'. Connectedness combines the indicators of cultural, economic, and political power that are embodied in the indicators of the publication of newspapers, the railway network, the concentration of corporate head offices, and the geographical origins of Members of Parliament. Each of the first three variables relates to access to the outside world while the fourth relates to the creation of local élites who are capable of influencing the country. One would expect this variable to be positively associated with support for the party of the core, namely the Conservative Party.

The second factor, 'marginalisation', combines the cultural traditions that result from a tendency to specialise in sheep farming with the economic stagnation that is reflected in high levels of out-migration. People who live in counties that score highly on this measure do not have a high degree of influence over the outside world; in fact, many are leaving to seek better prospects elsewhere. One would expect that such residents

FIGURE 5.7
CORE AND PERIPHERY IN 1891, 1921, 1951 AND 1991

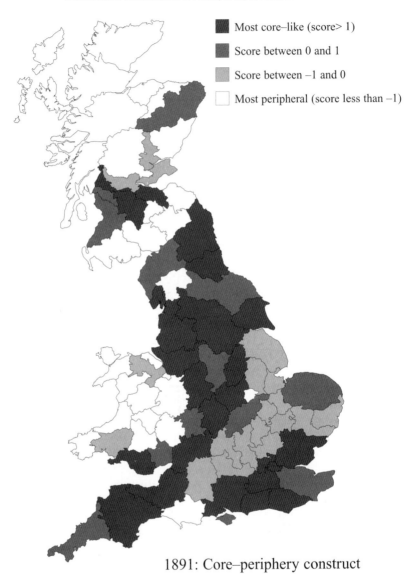

■ Most core–like (score> 1)

■ Score between 0 and 1

░ Score between –1 and 0

□ Most peripheral (score less than –1)

1891: Core–periphery construct

FIGURE 5.7 (continued)
CORE AND PERIPHERY IN 1891, 1921, 1951 AND 1991

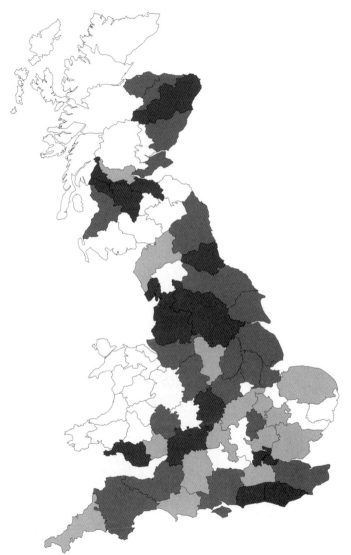

1921: Connectedness variable

FIGURE 5.7 (continued)
CORE AND PERIPHERY IN 1891, 1921, 1951 AND 1991

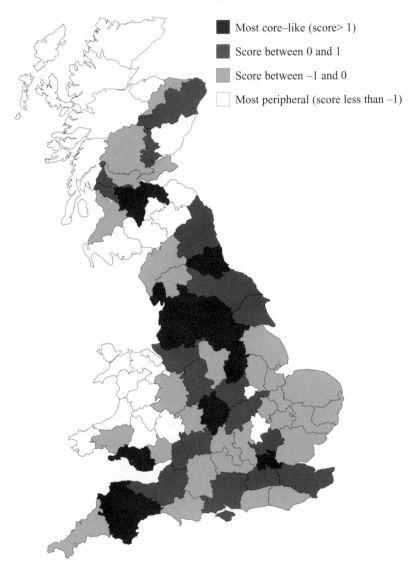

■ Most core–like (score> 1)

■ Score between 0 and 1

■ Score between –1 and 0

□ Most peripheral (score less than –1)

1951: Connectedness variable

FIGURE 5.7 (continued)
CORE AND PERIPHERY IN 1891, 1921, 1951 AND 1991

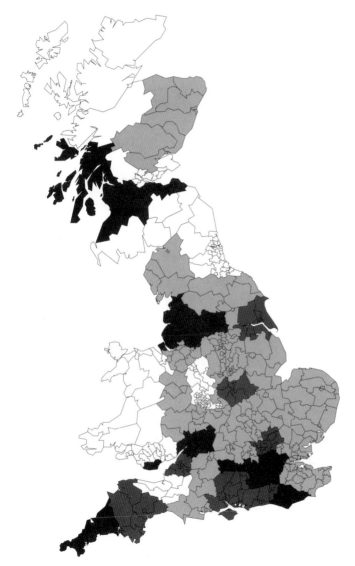

1991: Connectedness variable

would prefer parties that stand in opposition to the Conservatives. This is not to say that they would necessarily vote Labour; only that they would be less likely to support the Conservatives.

The geographic distribution of core and periphery in 1891 and 'connectedness' in 1921, 1951 and 1991, can be compared in Figure 5.7. In 1891 the areas scoring highest on the scale included the major cities (London, Birmingham, Manchester, Liverpool, Hull, Gloucester, Edinburgh, Glasgow, and Cardiff), much of the south-east, and parts of industrial England. Least core-like areas included rural Wales, most of Scotland, and much of rural England. By 1921 many more areas had a level of 'connectedness' that placed them in the core: north-east Scotland, Lincolnshire, and Fife, for example, while the south-east exhibited fewer core characteristics than hitherto. The same was true for 1951: the distribution of core areas was more diffuse than in 1891. The final period, as expected, concentrated core areas again in the south-east and the largest cities.[29] Wales and northernmost England fell decidedly into the periphery, as did Fife, Staffordshire and the West Midlands. As with the individual characteristics explored above, a visual inspection of the core–periphery continuum suggests that Britain has indeed conformed to the model projected at the outset of this essay.

ELECTION RESULTS: TESTING THE DYNAMIC MODEL

The substantial changes in county and local government boundaries that took effect with the 1974 elections and the 1981 census make comparisons with the models and elections of earlier years rather difficult. It is possible to fit pre- and post-reorganisation counties into nearly constant boundaries, but the result is a very small number of units for analysis with a limited number of boundary problems. These problems, combined with the small number of observations, reduce the validity of the regression equations while artificially inflating $R^2$ coefficients.[30] With this in mind, the discussion of election results begins with the election of January 1910, proceeds to 1922 and 1951, and concludes with 1992.

The January 1910 election was geographically the most polarised of the pre-war contests. Class, religion, and the core–periphery construct combine to explain 62 per cent of the variance in the Conservative/Unionist vote at that election. All independent variables are statistically significant estimators of the Conservative and Unionist vote on that occasion. Standardised regression coefficients for the equation are presented in Table 5.2. Repeating the computations using the 1910 election data and the same socio-economic data while substituting first the 1921 and then the 1951 core–periphery conceptualisations shows that neither of these models is statistically significant: core and periphery as defined in 1921 and 1951 are not useful for estimating the Unionist vote in January 1910. The failure of these models provides strong support for the initial hypothesis that electoral change followed changes in the positions of the counties of Britain on the continuum.

The inter-war period was marked by considerable electoral turbulence both within the opposition Liberal and Labour Parties and across the core–periphery cleavage. Table 5.3 compares the impact that changing patterns of core and periphery had on estimates of the Conservative vote in 1921. Each column regresses the vote on variables identified as critical to the Party's support: its core class (employers and managers) and agriculture.[31] The first column uses only these variables; the resulting $R^2$ is low at 0.21. The second column adds the core–periphery variable from the 1891 model. The variable is a useful addition, but the increase in predictive capacity ($R^2 = 0.23$) is quite small. The 1891 model does explain the 1921 election very well.

The third column regresses the 1922 Conservative vote on class, agriculture, and the 1921 core–periphery model, while the fourth column substitutes the 1951 model in an otherwise identical regression equation. Both conceptualisations add significantly to the understanding of this election: the most important influence on the 1922 Conservative vote was class, followed by marginalisation and connectedness, while agriculture was not useful. Conservative support in 1922 was higher in areas of more political and economic power, and in areas where migration and the way of life were more outward-looking in their orientation.

TABLE 5.2
EXPLAINING THE CONSERVATIVE VOTE, JANUARY 1910

| | Core–periphery measure | | |
|---|---|---|---|
| | 1891 | 1921 | 1951 |
| Nonconformity | −0.43* | −0.25* | −0.23* |
| Anglicanism | 0.32* | 0.26* | 0.26* |
| Roman Catholicism | 0.28* | 0.22* | 0.26* |
| Class | −0.29* | −0.22* | −0.21 |
| Core–periphery (1891) | 0.19* | – | – |
| Connectedness | – | 0.15 | 0.20 |
| Marginalisation | – | 0.15 | 0.05 |
| Constant | 0.48 | 0.41 | 0.39 |
| $R^2$ | 0.62 | 0.36 | 0.34 |
| N | 116 | 116 | 116 |

The measure used for Nonconformity is the percentage of the population attending Sunday school in 1851. The variable for Anglicanism represents Anglican clergymen as a percentage of the 1891 adult male population. The percentage of the adult male population who were members of the Roman Catholic clergy in 1891 is used as the indicator of Roman Catholicism. The class variable is measured as the percentage of the 1901 labour force that was unionised. For details, see K. Wald, *Crosses on the Ballot* (Princeton: Princeton University Press, 1983), Chapters 4 and 6.
Source: Compiled from data provided by Kenneth Wald.
* Significant at $\alpha = 0.05$ (two-tailed).

The final column in the table regresses the 1922 Conservative vote on class, agriculture, and the 1991 core–periphery model. The 1991 model is better than the 1891 model, as suggested by a comparison of the $R^2$ and the regression coefficients, but it is much less useful than either the 1921 or the 1951 model. Again, there is strong confirmation for the hypothesis that electoral support has varied across the country according to changes in the distribution of power.

Regression models for the 1951 Conservative vote use the same social class and agriculture variables as the 1922 regressions in Table 5.3. The analysis for the 1951 election, given in Table 5.4, shows the 1951 model to be the best predictor of the Conservative vote. Not only is the sign for the 1921 'connectedness' variable in the wrong direction, suggesting that the Conservative vote *falls* as a county more closely approximates the core ideal, but neither conceptuali-

TABLE 5.3
COMPARING DYNAMIC MODELS:
Conservative Share of the 1922 Vote Regressed on Core–Periphery Models

| Variable list | no core–periphery measure | 1891 core–periphery | 1921 core–periphery | 1951 core–periphery | 1991 core–periphery |
|---|---|---|---|---|---|
| Class | 0.48* | 0.46* | 0.43* | 0.33* | 0.44* |
| Agriculture | –0.37* | –0.28* | –0.11 | –0.13 | –0.12 |
| 1891 core–periphery | – | 0.17* | – | – | – |
| Connectedness | – | – | 0.24* | 0.46* | –0.20 |
| Marginalisation | – | – | 0.41* | 0.53 | –0.51* |
| Constant | 0.14 | 0.13 | 0.13 | 0.15 | 0.11 |
| $R^2$ | 0.21 | 0.23 | 0.37 | 0.40 | 0.29 |

N=161.

Class is defined as the percentage of men employed as employers and managers from the 1966 census. Agriculture is defined as the percentage of men engaged in agriculture from the 1931 census. Connectedness and marginalisation are defined as in the text above.
* Significant at $\alpha=0.05$ (two-tailed).
Source: Calculated from W. L. Miller, *Electoral Dynamics Files, 1918-1979* (computer file) (Colchester: ESRC Data Archive) and data described in the Appendix.

sation of the continuum significantly adds to the predictive power of the equation. The 1991 model is as good as the 1951 model, but the signs on both the 'connectedness' and the 'marginalisation' parts of the measure are in the wrong direction. Again, this suggests that the Conservatives are more successful in the periphery than the core, which runs counter to the hypothesis and evidence presented elsewhere.[32] The 1951 model estimates the Conservative vote correctly as being positively related to the marginalisation construct – in other words Conservative support was higher in counties that experienced population gains through migration and in areas where the lower tendency to engage in sheep farming reflected a more outward-looking world view.

The 1992 election, the equations of which are in Table 5.5, suggests that Conservative support was higher in constituencies with more employers and managers, farmers, and connections with the rest of the world (connectedness),

TABLE 5.4
COMPARING DYNAMIC MODELS:
Conservative Share of the 1951 Vote Regressed on Core–Periphery Models

| Variable list | 1951 core–periphery | 1921 core–periphery | 1991 core–periphery |
|---|---|---|---|
| Class | 0.62* | 0.67* | 0.69* |
| Agriculture | –0.08 | –0.12 | –0.05 |
| Connectedness | 0.03 | –0.09 | –0.35* |
| Marginalisation | 0.24* | 0.07 | –0.35* |
| Constant | 0.22 | 0.21 | 0.20 |
| $R^2$ | 0.44 | 0.41 | 0.44 |

Source: Calculated from Miller, *Electoral Dynamics* (computer file) and data described in text.

but that it *decreases* as the constituency achieves more of the core ideal in terms of the 'marginalisation' variable. This is the only instance where regression analysis has failed to provide strong support for the hypotheses under investigation. The 'wrong' direction of association is probably due to the role that suburban voters have played as they move further and further away from cities. The rise of this urban-rural divide is a well-known phenomenon that has been explored elsewhere and does not invalidate the results of this analysis.[33] Core and

TABLE 5.5
COMPARING DYNAMIC MODELS:
Conservative Share of the Vote in 1992 Regressed on Core–Periphery Models

| Variable list | 1991 model | No core–periphery measure |
|---|---|---|
| Class | 0.65* | 0.73* |
| Agriculture | 0.30* | 0.35* |
| Connectedness 1951 | – | – |
| Marginalisation 1951 | – | – |
| Connectedness 1991 | 0.15* | – |
| Marginalisation 1991 | –0.25* | – |
| Constant | 7.83 | 3.47 |
| $R^2$ | 0.67 | 0.63 |

Source: Calculated from I. McAllister and R. Rose, *United Kingdom Ecological Data 1983, 1987* (machine readable file) (Colchester: ESRC Data Archive, 1987); *The Times Guide to the House of Commons 1992* (London: Times Newspapers Ltd, 1992); and data described in text and in the Appendix.

periphery add significantly to the predictive power of the regression equation to estimate the Conservative share of the vote at the 1992 British general election.

## SUMMARY

The dynamic core–periphery model fits the regional pattern of British voting behaviour remarkably well over the period studied. The periods when the Conservative vote has been regionally concentrated, the Edwardian era and the post-Butskellite era, are also periods when the country has been more sharply divided along core–periphery power measures. The electoral fortunes of the Conservative Party have varied in no small part because the structure of the British economy has changed to put certain regions and counties more-or-less in the core and others more-or-less in the periphery. As regions and counties shift, the voters respond with more or fewer votes for the party of the core.

The evidence above provides an answer to the question of the source of long-term geographical change in the British electorate. The Conservative Party is 'the party of King and Country', and voters respond to it on the basis of their structural position on the core–periphery cleavage. This effect is independent of occupational and employment status. The Conservative Party performs better in what is normally labelled the periphery when the actual cleavage line does not match the national boundaries between England, Wales, and Scotland, and when the southern borders of Lancashire and Yorkshire do not present such a stark delineation between core and periphery. On the other side of the cleavage, Labour and the Liberals are able to extend their reach further into what is generally thought of as the core when, as in the 1920s and 1950s, core and periphery are less clearly differentiated.

NOTES

1. J. R. Owens and L. L. Wade, 'Economic Conditions and Constituency Voting in Great Britain', *Political Studies*, 36, 1 (January 1988) pp. 30–51.

2. J. Galtung, 'A Structural Theory of Imperialism', *Journal of Peace Research*, 8 (1971) p. 104.

3. A. O. Hirschman, *Exit, Voice, and Loyalty; Responses to Decline in Firms, Organizations, and States* (Cambridge, MA: Harvard University Press, 1970).

4. W. L. Miller, *Electoral Dynamics in Britain Since 1918* (London: Macmillan, 1977).

5. K. D. Wald, *Crosses on the Ballot: Patterns of British Voter Alignment Since 1885* (Princeton: Princeton University Press, 1983).

6. Analysis of the 1987 British Election Survey suggests that social change boosted the Conservative vote by under three per cent and reduced the Labour vote by four per cent in 1987 relative to 1964. See A. F. Heath, R. Jowell, J. Curtice, G. Evans, J. Field, and S. Witherspoon, *Understanding Political Change: The British Voter, 1964-1987* (Oxford: Pergamon Press, 1991) p. 220.

7. Board of Agriculture, *Agricultural Returns of Great Britain with Abstract Returns for the United Kingdom, British Possessions, and Foreign Countries* (London: HMSO, 1891) p. 4.

8. P. L. Garside, 'London and the Home Counties', in F. M. L. Thompson (ed.), *The Cambridge Social History of Britain 1750-1950. Volume 1: Regions and Communities* (Cambridge: Cambridge University Press, 1990) pp. 476-80.

9. R. E. Crum and G. Gudgin, *Non-Production Activities in UK Manufacturing Industry* (Brussels: Commission of the European Community, 1977) p. 100.

10. Socio-economic groups 2 (employers and managers in industry, commerce, and establishments) and 4 (professional workers – employees).

11. H. D. Watts, 'Non-financial Head Offices: A View from the North', in J. Lewis and A. Townsend (eds) *The North–South Divide: Regional Change in Britain in the 1980s* (London: Paul Chapman, 1989) pp. 159–60.

12. M. J. Healey and H. D. Watts, 'The Multi-Plant Enterprise', in W. F. Lever (ed.), *Industrial Change in the United Kingdom* (London: Longman, 1987).

13. W. L. Miller, *The End of British Politics? Scots and English Political Behaviour in the Seventies* (Oxford: Clarendon Press, 1981) pp. 19–21.

14. Full details and sources are presented in the Appendix.

15. The method for determining MPs' origins is detailed in the Appendix.

16. The British Candidate Study, 1992, was directed by Professor Joni Lovenduski (Southampton University) and Dr Pippa Norris (Harvard University). The study was funded by the Economic and Social Research Council (R000-23-1991). The author gratefully acknowledges the permission given by Dr Norris and Professor Lovenduski to use this study and absolves them of responsibility for any misinterpretations of the data.

17. D. A. Irwin, 'The Politics of Free Trade: Voting in the British General Election of 1906', *Journal of Law and Economics*, 37, 1 (April 1994) pp. 75–108; D. A. Irwin, 'Industry or Class Cleavages over Trade Policy? Evidence from the British General Election of 1923', National Bureau of Economic Research, Inc., Working Paper No. 5170, 1995.

18. E. A. Wrigley, 'A Simple Model of London's Importance in Changing English Society and Economy 1650–1750', *Past and Present*, 37 (1967) pp. 44–70.

19. P. L. Garside, pp. 472-80.

20. F. M. L. Thompson, 'Town and City', in F. M. L. Thompson (ed.), *The Cambridge Social History of Britain 1750–1950. Volume I: Regions and*

*Communities* (Cambridge: Cambridge University Press, 1990) p. 55.

21. N. Thrift, A. Leyshon, and P. Daniels, *Sexy Greedy: The New International Financial System, the City of London, and the Southeast of England* (University of Bristol and University of Liverpool: Working Papers on Producer Services No. 8, 1987); A. Leyshon and N. Thrift, 'South Goes North? The Rise of the British Provincial Financial Centre', in J. Lewis and A. Townsend (eds), *The North–South Divide: Regional Change in Britain in the 1980s* (London: Paul Chapman, 1989) p. 118.

22. Because there was no census held in 1941, the 1951 census reports migration over the preceding 20 years.

23. In all periods, population change due to migration includes military deaths overseas.

24. Y. Saueressig-Schreuder, 'The Impact of British Colonial Rule on the Urban Hierarchy of Burma', *Review*, 2 (Fall 1986) pp. 245–77.

25. See, for example, R. Melson and H. Wolpe, 'Modernization and the Politics of Communication: A Theoretical Perspective', *American Political Science Review*, 64, 4 (December 1970) pp. 1112–30.

26. F. Barth, *Ethnic Groups and Boundaries: The Social Organization of Cultural Difference* (Boston: Little, Brown, 1969) pp. 9–38.

27. J. Galtung, p. 100.

28. The z-score 'is used in statistics to express the distance between a number $Y$ and the mean $\mu$ of a probability distribution, in terms of the number of standard deviations that $Y$ is from $\mu$'. See A. Agresti and B. Finlay, *Statistical Methods for the Social Sciences*, 2nd edition (San Francisco: Dellen Publishing, 1986) p. 74.

29. Boundary changes create a certain confusion in the Strathclyde region. In the first three-sample period Glasgow's pre-eminence was limited to Lanarkshire, but reorganisation of local government in the 1970s places nearly all of the old Highlands county of Argyll in Glasgow's orbit. The apparent size of the Scottish core is deceptively enlarged as a result.

30. For a discussion of these problems, see V. Bogdanor and W. H. Field, 'Lessons of History: Core and Periphery in British Electoral Behaviour, 1910–1992', *Electoral Studies*, 12, 3 (September 1993) pp. 204–24.

31. For a discussion of these variables and the adequacy of using the 1966 census for the 1922 election, see W. L. Miller, 1977.

32. See especially W. L. Miller, 'The De-Nationalisation of British Politics: The Re-Emergence of the Periphery', *West European Politics*, 6, 4 (October, 1983) pp. 103–29.

33. See, for example, J. Curtice and M. Steed, 'Proportionality and Exaggeration in the British Electoral System', *Electoral Studies*, 5, 3 (December 1986) pp. 209–28.

# CHAPTER SIX

# Stability in Change in British Politics

THE ACCEPTED view of British electoral developments has viewed Britain as a country whose nineteenth century political parties were constrained by religious differences, but whose politics have more recently moved to a cleavage structure based on social class. Whereas the great divide in the late Victorian and Edwardian years was between Anglican Conservatives and anti-Anglican Nonconformist Liberals, the defining quality of politics in the heyday of the Westminster model was always assumed to be class: manual workers for the Labour Party and everyone else for the Conservatives.

## A STRUCTURED POLITY

Recent electoral developments have come to challenge that view. There is some evidence that the class cleavage is weakening and there is also a growing polarisation of electoral support between the south-east of England and the north, Scotland, and Wales. The electorate is now generally understood to be regionally based with economic conditions affecting the distribution at the margins.[1]

In Chapter Two, a brief electoral history of Britain showed that, far from being new, the north–south divide bears a certain resemblance to the electoral geography of the Edwardian years, and especially to the January 1910 election. This finding raised the possibility that the current period has been influenced by similar structural forces to those that influenced the Edwardian period. On the surface, however, such a hypothesis appeared implausible; religion is not now as important, politically or socially, as it was a century ago.

The political issues that were raised in the last decade of the nineteenth century and the first decade of this one suggest that religion was not in fact the driving structure often assumed by most observers. In fact, the Anglican–Nonconformist disputes were decidedly of a core–periphery character and were not strictly based on theological differences. This is especially true of the most geographically polarised election of that period: January 1910. Issues from the status of Ireland and of the Church in Wales, to the role of the House of Lords, and to state funding for church schools, revolved primarily around the argument of local control versus central control. Religion was an important element of the debate, but it was primarily a tool for crafting arguments. Having discovered the extent of the core–periphery alignment in the Edwardian period, the question arose whether similar issues had been gaining influence in shaping elections in the 1980s and 1990s.

The degree of regional change in patterns of electoral support suggests that, for Britain, Stein Rokkan's famous freezing hypothesis is incorrect. For an electorate to be frozen, there must be little movement in the geographic distribution of electoral strength. On the surface, the regional swings in England, Scotland, and Wales do not lend support to this hypothesis. The re-emergence of a north–south divide after a 30- to 50-year period when there was only minimal regional polarisation suggests that the British electorate has been in constant, but relatively slow, flux. The old core–periphery cleavage that structured late Victorian and Edwardian politics appears to have re-emerged.

## The core–periphery influence

The core–periphery explanation for the north–south divide stands in great contrast to the economic voting that underpins our understanding of recent elections. To be accepted as plausible, alternative explanations must be shown to be less robust in explanatory power. In Chapter Three we saw that the economic and social identity models of voting behaviour were incomplete as explanations for the rising disparity of support between north and south. A regional dimension of party support has risen since 1959 that does not fit well into either approach.

In place of these incomplete explanations, and as an expanded element of the social identity model, the concepts of core and periphery were introduced in Chapter Four to provide an alternative cleavage to class around which voters could structure their electoral preferences. The chapter offered two definitions of core and periphery. The traditional conceptualisation, here called the static model, is based on the permanent placement of counties on one side or the other of the divide. This model cannot account for changes in the salience of a cleavage over time, so a dynamic model was introduced where certain core–periphery indicators could be measured to develop a composite score for a core–periphery construct. In contrast to the fixed nature of the static model, this dynamic approach allowed for a fluid definition of core and periphery: counties could be placed on one side of the cleavage at one point in time, and on the other side at a different point. The model also allowed for the degree of difference between counties to increase and decrease, suggesting thereby that the core–periphery cleavage could become more or less salient over time.

In Chapter Five the dynamic model was developed and tested. Six elements of the British socio-political economy were measured at four different points in time: in 1891, 1921, 1951, and 1991. These were then combined into core–periphery constructs which were used to estimate Conservative Party support in 1910, 1922, 1951, and 1992. Factors that have been recognised as influential over the years were also included: religion and class in 1910, class and agricultural employment in the years since then. Several conclusions were drawn from the geographical distribution of the constructs and from the impact of the variables on estimates of the Conservative vote in the regression models.

- *Construct validity.* The constructs did indeed measure the core–periphery cleavage. London scored highest at all four time periods, while the Scottish Highlands uniformly scored the lowest. As expected, London appeared as the heart of Britain, the most core area, year after year. In contrast, the Scottish Highlands were, as is generally accepted, the most peripheral parts of Great Britain. In terms of the structure of the British polity, these are the poles. Other parts of Britain generally scored more-or-less as expected.

- *Cleavage variability.* This cleavage varied somewhat from period to period of measurement. While many counties did not shift between core and periphery, variations in scores between counties in one year and in the same county across years suggested both a spatial component and a dynamic element to the constructs.

- *Conservative core.* The electoral base of the Conservative Party lies in the core, not in the periphery. Macaulay's description of the Anglican Church as the Tory party at prayer is correct in so far as this church is the religious expression of the core. There is a fundamental equality between the Conservatives, the Anglican Church, and the monarchy.

- *Useful analysis.* The constructs were useful for predicting the distribution of support for the Conservative Party. Each of the four time-bound models was successful in adding predictive capacity to regression equations of party support at the elections closest to the sampling year. In particular,

  1. The 1891 construct contributed more to the explanation of Conservative support in 1910 than did any other.

  2. While earlier analyses had not shown a significant regional dimension of support for the party of the core during the inter-war and immediate post-war periods, this was not confirmed here. On the contrary, the 1921 and 1951 models suggested that there *was* spatial

variation in voting in the inter-war elections that could be tied to a core–periphery cleavage. Contrary to widespread belief, core and periphery did not disappear during this period; the geographic base and socio-economic salience of the cleavage shifted, and the cultural and economic structures that define the periphery became more diffuse in their distribution, making the regional distinction between core and periphery less apparent.

3. The success of the 1991 model to predict the 1992 election, when the 1951 model failed, shows the widening north–south divide of the 1959 to 1987 period (with a slight reversal in 1992) has a base in the structural changes in the country.

- *No weakening of the class cleavage.* There was no evidence to support the hypothesis of a weakening class cleavage at the aggregate level. Since the core–periphery constructs were approximately equal in their influence in terms of increases in predictive capacity (through the $R^2$), a weakening of the class cleavage is not necessary to produce rising regional polarisation. The class cleavage may indeed be losing its influence, but that is a separate debate.

To summarise, British electoral developments have indeed been shaped by core and periphery. The north–south divide is not inexplicable.

## Model building

This analysis relating core and periphery to voting patterns mixes some elements from the two main models of electoral choice. The core–periphery model is a structural model. As developed in these pages it places greatest weight on an economic model of Britain, but one that is based more on long-term, structural change than on short-term performance fluctuations. Counties were placed in the core at least partially on the strength of their economic performance over the previous decade. At the same time, the model draws on more enduring structures that shape the British political space. Railway systems do not change overnight; neither do population growth patterns, farming practices, nor the distribution of corporate head office locations. As with weather forecasting, the safest prediction to make about these surrogate measures for the core–periphery dimension is one of stability from year to year and decade to decade.

While capturing stability, these indicators also measure change in the distribution of counties along the core–periphery axis. Today's suburban London has shifted from being a 'backwater to the city', and therefore slightly in the periphery, to a core position second only to London itself. In this context, it is simple to explain the development of an overwhelming Conservative hegemony in the south-east. People select the party of the core because they are connected to the core, and to the power structures that mark the core, not because they have a sense of belonging to the core, or have allegiance to some core ideal. The opposite is true in the peripheries: industrial Lancashire and Yorkshire, for example, are more peripheral in terms of economic, political, and cultural power than in the 1920s or even the 1890s, and the voting patterns reflect this. Other parts of Britain have also changed their core–periphery status. Scotland has lost considerable power and influence to the south, and support for the Conservative Party has fallen commensurably.

The development of a dynamic model relating tangible indicators of economic and social conditions to the vote marks an improvement over models that divide Britain into static core and periphery areas, or into three nations, because the model develops a plausible hypothesis about why different parts of Britain should vote as they do. As such, core and periphery can now be placed alongside class, education, and housing tenure, as a predictor of the British vote.

Unlike these other variables, which affect voting because of the direct placement of the individual in a group, core and periphery offers a context to the electoral decision. When voters choose a party contrary to their natural class preferences it is not because they live in Scotland or the north of England, for example, but because of their connections to the core. Over time, the allegiance of voters deviates more-or-less from their natural class party in part because their perceived interests change in tandem with changes in the extent of the local power structure. Core and periphery introduce a structural element to the electoral model which is absent or ill-defined in standard economic or sociological models of the vote. Regionalism need no longer be a historical anomaly; it may be carefully and concisely defined in its effects.

## IMPLICATIONS

The existence of an evolving core–periphery influence on the British electorate poses questions for past and future. To some extent, the core–periphery dynamic offers a new explanation for the collapse of the Liberal Party during the 1920s. It also suggests what could happen to Labour if the structure of the British state changes in reaction to the nationalist demands from Scotland and Wales or to increased powers at the European level. At a different level, knowledge of the changing nature of this cleavage could suggest that certain policy options would further the electoral hopes of the main parties, while other options would be detrimental.

### Party system effects

The near-simultaneous occurrence of the collapse of the Liberal Party with a reduction in the salience of the core–periphery cleavage suggests an alternative explanation to 'the strange death of Liberal England'. It is worth noting that, with very few exceptions, all of the Liberal governments since 1832 existed on the sufferance of the periphery, first from Liberal seats in Ireland, then from Irish Nationalists. As we saw in Chapter Two, many of the issues that the Liberals used to rally support revolved around Irish Home Rule. With the departure of Ireland from the United Kingdom, support for the primary party of the periphery fell below a sufficient level to form a government. Torn by internecine squabbles, the party soon neared oblivion.

Although Labour is not primarily a party of the periphery, its geography of support is biased away from the core. Recollecting the fate of the Liberals, whose government between 1910 and 1915 depended on 84 Irish Nationalist seats, we can extrapolate to the present position of the Labour Party. If the removal of Ireland, and of issues concerning Ireland, helped destroy the Liberals, then the removal of Scotland is likely to severely damage Labour. Labour is advocating, among other things, the establishment of a Scottish Assembly and the transfer of considerable power to lower levels than the Westminster Parliament. While the party would probably not suffer as seriously as did the Liberals, devolution would reduce Labour's representation at Westminster and also eliminate much of the sectional basis of its support. Despite the party's apparent lead in recent opinion polls, Labour's chance to build a governing majority might well vanish following serious devolution. Barring a major catastrophe for the party of the core, current trends suggest the Conservatives would inherit a perpetual majority.

Because of the way parties align along the core–periphery cleavage, a change in the underlying *raison d'être* of that cleavage, such as Scottish devolution or independence, would have significant consequences on the British party system. What would devolution do to the core–periphery cleavage itself? What would be the consequences, for example, of Scotland's entering the European Union as an independent country?

### Cleavage effects

A core needs a periphery; otherwise it is not a core. The loss of empire cost London considerable political and economic stature in the world. Where the financial prowess of the City of London far exceeded the mobilisable resources of any other core in the late nineteenth century, the City today has much less influence over world affairs. Decisions that, a hundred years ago, would have been made completely within London's square mile are now being made in New York, Washington, Geneva, and Tokyo, at least as often as in London. A further reduction in the reach of the London core would similarly reduce the city's influence in the world.

Three scenarios in the structural make-up of Britain are possible. The country could continue unchanged, devolve power to Scotland, Wales, and perhaps English regions, or could grant outright independence to Scotland. The Conservative Party's preferred outcome is, of course, no change. Once it has recovered from its current low rating in the opinion polls, the Conservatives could expect to lose nearly all representation in the periphery, especially Scotland, while regaining its overwhelming dominance in the core. The result: once the party's current woes have been overcome there would be Conservative hegemony for the foreseeable future. This would especially be true if Labour won the next election and failed to respond to periphery demands for more self-government. Labour would lose support to the Scottish Nationalists, the Liberal Democrats, and perhaps Plaid Cymru in a way that would seriously undermine its re-election chances.

Simple devolution would have no effect on the geography of the core–periphery cleavage. The Scots would still vote for the Westminster Parliament (although probably electing fewer MPs), and decisions taken in London would still affect Scotland. Economically and culturally, the Scottish, Welsh, and English components of the periphery would still exist in tandem and in contrast to the English core. Devolution would be the best outcome for Labour, which could point to the satisfaction of peripheral grievances without losing a critical electoral base. Nationalist and Liberal Democrat sentiment might well fade as the parties lose some of their political rationale. Devolution would be the worst outcome for the Conservatives.

The same cannot be said for Scottish independence. The increased cultural homogeneity of England and Wales that would result from the full independence of Scotland would accentuate the political and cultural differences between the south-east and northern England. The gulf between Yorkshiremen and those 'foreign' southerners would remain, with all the differences in voting propensity that exist now. On the other hand, the boundary between core and periphery might possibly shift somewhat to the south. People in the Midlands who currently feel more connected to

London may find themselves becoming more marginalised. People might change their party allegiance somewhat in consequence. The size of the core might shrink.

Full independence for Scotland would guarantee Conservative supremacy indefinitely once the party's current troubles were past. As such, following this strategy makes the most electoral sense for the party. All non-Conservative parties (except Plaid Cymru) would lose representation, and it would take many years for them to build support farther south, even if the English periphery expanded. While this strategy goes against the Conservative's One-Nation beliefs, Scottish independence would be an outcome that Conservative leaders could tacitly favour.

An analogy can be drawn with the politics of the repeal of the Corn Laws. The landed interests that stood behind the Conservative Party in the 1840s were virulently opposed to repeal, yet Conservatives who had been members of Sir Robert Peel's government saw the sense in it.[2] Knowing that repeal would temporarily disrupt the party, they still saw, correctly, that the policy would eventually work to the Conservatives' benefit.

The same is true for Scotland today. The granting of Scottish independence would alienate many One-Nation Tories in the south of England but there is no alternative party to which they can turn. A more imperialist party (such as the British Empire Party of 1951) might arise, but its electoral success is likely to be small and ephemeral. While a Conservative split is possible, it is likely to occur over the proper British approach to the European Union, not devolution or Scottish independence. After a period of confusion, the Conservatives would emerge strengthened.

The same cannot be said for Labour. Scotland's small constituencies provide Labour with an inordinate level of parliamentary support. Were the number of Scottish seats in Westminster to be reduced to make their electorates comparable in size to those of the English constituencies, Labour's chance of achieving a parliamentary majority would be severely diminished. Labour's position as a party *in* the periphery, but not *of* the periphery, is very awkward.

Members of the Scottish Labour Party may find the

consolation prize, Labour governance in Scotland with additional influence in the European Commission, enough to compensate for their loss in Westminster. Nevertheless, members of the Party further south would find little solace in this outcome. The best option for the party would be to position itself more clearly as a party *of* the *core* (much as Jo Grimond tried to reposition the Liberals in the 1950s) and to rally support in the Midlands. A shift in the core–periphery boundary, which might happen should Scotland achieve full independence, would aid Labour efforts in this direction. The choice of Tony Blair, Member for Sedgefield, as party leader is a good first step,[3] but making the party leadership more English would be even better.

The real winners of devolution in Scotland would be the Liberal Democrats. With the chance to hold the reins of power, the Scottish Nationalists would again be seen to have little to offer the electorate other than self-government. With that achieved, disaffected voters could then turn back to the Liberal Democrats and divide the Scottish political system between themselves and Labour. A similar outcome might occur in Wales, given a Welsh Assembly, but further Liberal success in peripheral England appears unlikely at this time.

If the centrifugal forces of increasing regional polarisation have their way and devolution or independence come to Scotland and Wales, the effects on the distribution of party support would be great. While the cleavage structures themselves would not change significantly, except in the case of full independence for Scotland, the spatial distribution of party support might be significantly altered. Party leaders and thinkers are well advised to take the core–periphery cleavage into account when planning policy positions and electoral strategy in the coming years.

## Effecting change: political influence over the cleavage

Politics is not exclusively *dependent* on social structure and economic forces; political outcomes can also *change* structures. If there is one lesson to be learned from a renewed focus on political institutions, it is that they are not captive creatures of their environment.[4] The contemporary structure of the

American West is substantially the result of federal government policies regarding land grants (homesteading), railway rights of way, and military occupation. The social structure of Britain has been similarly affected: the transformation of ten per cent of the housing stock from public to private ownership, through the council-house sales programme, resulted from political decisions dating from the early to mid-1970s.[5]

The core–periphery cleavage has had considerable influence over electoral events in Britain. To a great extent this influence has been beyond any political control. However, there are policy options that might help a party's standing in the core–periphery cleavage short of advocating continued unity for Britain, devolution to lower tiers of government, or outright independence for Scotland and/or Wales. As suggested above, these policies would have substantial implications on the electoral fortunes of the main parties as a result of their influence on the translation of the core–periphery cleavage into parliamentary representation. Other policies may have positive or negative ramifications too.

*Policy options for the Conservatives*
The most obvious policy choice, regional aid, has already been tried. Despite differences in per capita income between London and Glasgow that are far smaller than differences between Paris and Marseilles, or between Turin and Palermo,[6] and despite over four decades of regional aid granted by both Conservative and Labour governments, the north–south divide expanded. Another likely policy failure is the distribution of government offices across Britain. The Scottish and the Welsh Office both gained substantial powers in the years since 1945, yet, again, the north–south divide has re-emerged. Quick fixes, whether in terms of the granting of financial incentives or the relocation of government agencies, have not worked in the past, and are not likely to work in the future.

The most likely area where a Conservative government could reverse the north–south divide is through a reduction in central control over local government. This is an area that has not been fully explored in these pages, but local government represents an important symbol of local control. In France a response to demands for devolution has been the replacement of appointed local government officials with elected officials; in Britain one response under Conservative governments since 1979 has been the forced emasculation of local government powers, through new regulations, school and health service opt-outs, rate caps, and similar policies. Outside the granting of independence for Scotland, discussed above, policies aimed at encouraging local government innovation and independence would have a spill-over effect on Conservative support in parliamentary elections.

*Policy options for Labour*

If Labour succeeds in forming a government, its policies should be aimed at increasing the north–south divide while moving the boundary further south. This is difficult; most of the policies that a Labour government might advocate – devolving power to Scotland, Wales, and the English regions – have the side-effect of making regions less distinct and thus making a Conservative government more palatable to voters in the periphery. If Labour has become a party *of* the periphery, as opposed to a party simply *in* the periphery, as suggested above, any policy it adopts to further the cause of the periphery carries with it the seeds of the party's destruction. The Liberals found this to their cost at the beginning of this century: the satisfaction of demands made by Nonconformists and the departure of Ireland from the United Kingdom were influential in causing the party's near-demise.

Labour's best option is to attempt to fight the Conservatives on economic rather than core–periphery issues. If the party can reinvigorate the class cleavage, while paying lip service to the periphery, it has the best chance of increasing its electoral base to include more of southern England. Otherwise, Tony Blair may well face a brief day in the sun as he presides over the demise of the party as a nationwide force in British politics.

## BENEFITS FROM THE CORE–PERIPHERY MODEL

The prime area where the development and deployment of a dynamic core–periphery model is beneficial lies in the interaction between the core–periphery matrix, on the one hand, and electoral results on the other. This reintroduction of institutional structures, of context, allows a more robust explanation for the rise of centrifugal political forces, such as separatist parties, in the periphery.

Other research has contributed a considerable amount of knowledge about regional dynamics. Johann Galtung's path-breaking essay on imperialism has laid out a framework for much analysis. This model has been employed in numerous articles. Surprisingly, however, little of the research has gone beyond describing the differences between core and periphery: there has been almost no effort to concretely specify *how much* cores and peripheries differ, or on drawing precise boundaries between core and periphery areas.[7] The only well-known study of regional variation in Britain that defines core and periphery in terms of an economic characteristic as opposed to a historically defined region, Hechter's *Internal Colonialism*,[8] contained a substantial error in its choice of distinguishing variable; as we have seen, the British core does not define itself according to levels of industrialisation.

Selecting a number of variables on a range of factors is more likely to achieve a correct specification of core and periphery than a model that equates industrial strength with the core. The identification of these variables marks a step, albeit perhaps a small one, toward a further understanding of the core–periphery dynamic and how it relates to political developments.

Identifying core–periphery variables, while important, is not the only contribution this study has made, however. There is a second area where the reader will find this analysis useful. Core and periphery have traditionally been seen as static concepts. The research agenda followed here has sought variables that distinguished core from periphery which could be repeatedly measured to build a model of *change:* changes in the salience of core and periphery, and in the boundary between them, feed into the electoral system. Chapter Five showed that the regional polarisation that marked electoral developments in the Edwardian period and the most recent decades did not disappear completely in the years between the First World War and 1959. The 1950s were not so much a period of national swing and national politics, as opposed to regional polarisation; the actual picture results from changes in the distribution of core and periphery that were reflected in the voting booth. In this sense, the regional dynamic that has run through British politics since the dawn of modern democracy in 1885 did not disappear but simply became less recognisable by conventional means. Institutional structures matter: a change in the organising structure of British society led to a change in the voting patterns. As the differences between core and periphery diminished or grew more diffuse, regional variation seemed to disappear. As these differences became more spatially concentrated again, regional variation, as measured conventionally, reappeared.

The major parties would be well advised to consider core–periphery effects when devising policy alternatives. Labour's successes have occurred when power has been most evenly distributed around the country, so the party should work to minimise geographical polarisation if and when it gains power. On the other hand, by playing on the core–periphery cleavage and the power differences that result, the Conservatives should be able to maintain their long-term dominance of British politics. The choice of party strategy and the evolution of the core–periphery dynamic will continue to have profound implications for Britain in the years to come.

NOTES

1. I. Crewe, P. Norris, and R. Waller, 'The 1992 General Election', in I. Crewe, P. Norris, D. Denver, and D. Broughton (eds), *British Elections and Parties Yearbook: 1992* (London: Harvester Wheatsheaf, 1992).
2. B. Disraeli, *Lord George Bentinck: A Political Biography* (London: Colburn and Company, 1852) pp. 299–300; W. O. Aydelotte, 'The Country Gentlemen and the Repeal of the Corn Laws', *English Historical Review*, 82 (1967) pp. 47–60.
3. The two preceding leaders were from Wales and Scotland.
4. This is well illustrated in P. A. Hall, *Governing the Economy: The Politics of State Intervention in Britain and France* (New York: Oxford University Press, 1986); and A. Lijphart, *Electoral Systems and Party Systems: A Study of Twenty-Seven*

*Democracies, 1945–1990* (Oxford: Oxford University Press, 1994) pp. 78–94.

5. W. H. Field, 'Council House Sales and Local Governments: A Case of Conflicting Goals', *Representation*, forthcoming.

6. J. Lewis and A. Townsend, 'Introduction', in J. Lewis and A. Townsend (eds), *The North–South Divide: Regional Change in Britain in the 1980s* (London: Paul Chapman, 1989) p. 6.

7. This is a direct result of the fact that much of the core–periphery literature has not dealt with the concepts as geographical facts, but simply as theoretical constructs. For a discussion, see E. S. Wellhofer, 'Core and Periphery: Territorial Dimensions in Politics', *Urban Studies* 26 (1989) p. 342.

8. M. Hechter, *Internal Colonialism: The Celtic Fringe in British National Development 1536–1966* (Berkeley and Los Angeles: University of California Press, 1975).

# The 1997 General Election in the Context of the Core–Periphery Continuum

ELIMINATED FROM Scotland and Wales. Reduced to 17 seats in the north of England. The Conservative electoral catastrophe that was the general election of 1997 struck far harder in what we commonly call peripheral Britain than in the core. However, while the Conservatives were humiliated all across the country, the election did little to reverse the north–south divide in a general shift towards Labour. Instead, 1997 saw the continued polarisation of Britain into two regionally concentrated and opposing camps.[1] The existence of a predominately Conservative core and a vehemently non-Conservative periphery continued. The Conservatives retained 41 per cent of the seats in the south of the country, but they won only seven per cent in the north. This brief post-election analysis will discuss the results of the 1997 election in the context of the core–periphery theory developed in the previous pages.

Despite the radical change in the composition of the House of Commons that resulted from the 1 May election, the 1997 results follow to a large extent the same pattern as those of 1992. The correlation of the geographic distribution of party support between 1992 and 1997 is as high as the correlation between 1987 and 1992.[2] This stability is far more typical of elections of the 1980s than of those of the more tumultuous 1920s, as a quick comparison with Table 2.3 will show. We can conclude from this that the Conservative defeat has more to do with a general withdrawal of support from the party than with a realignment of the electorate behind Labour.

A second comparison with past elections will show the extent to which the persistence of the north–south divide is reflected in the 1997 Parliament. There have been two non-Conservative landslides this century. In 1945, Labour took power on a platform promising to strengthen the welfare state, nationalise major industries and redistribute power across social classes. Core–periphery issues were irrelevant to that election and to the political debates that followed.

The landslide of 1906, on the other hand, occurred in the context of a generally widening regional electoral cleavage and increasing demands for a redistribution of power towards peripheral areas.[3] In that Liberal triumph, the Conservatives were beset with internal divisions over Free Trade that the Prime Minister, A. J. Balfour, was even less successful in overcoming than John Major has been on the issue of Europe.[4] The party was humiliated in 1906 as a result, and the divisions continued to trouble the party into the 1920s.

In 1906 the Conservative and Unionist vote collapsed both in the north and south of Britain, and stayed low in northern England, Scotland and Wales over the next four elections. In the south, however, Liberal plans to act on the core–periphery issues discussed in Chapter Two above galvanised voters into giving the Conservatives well over half the seats in the elections of 1910. By 1922, it was the Liberals who were demoralised, disorganised and facing oblivion, not the Conservatives.

The issues facing the newly elected government and opposition parties today are very similar to the period between 1906 and 1910. Devolution/Home Rule, electoral reform (including women's suffrage) and reform of the House of Lords were on the agenda of the 1906 Parliament. These were all issues of granting power to the powerless, and all but the suffrage are on the agenda of the 1997 Parliament. Labour's choices on these core–periphery issues are likely to increase Conservative support in core areas before the next election, while solidifying anti-Conservative support in the areas lacking in political, economic or social power that were discussed in Chapter Five. If the election of 1997 harkens back to 1906, then the next election may well have even more in common with 1910 than did the elections of 1987 and 1992.


## PITFALLS ON THE REPEAT OF HISTORY

Two pitfalls stand in the way of a repeat of 1910 in the general election of 2001–2002. The first is under the control of the governing Labour Party; the second depends on the reaction of the Conservatives to their electoral defeat and to their internal divisions.

Previous electoral reforms have often been neutral in their partisan influence or have actually benefited the Conservative Party.[5] The Conservatives were far more successful at mobilising new voters after the nineteenth-century expansions of the franchise, while the redistributions of seats this century have usually increased representation in Conservative areas to the detriment of non-Conservative areas suffering population loss.[6] Outweighing all other electoral reforms since 1918, however, is the impact that would result from Labour bowing to Liberal Democrat demands and introducing some form of proportional representation. If this were to happen, then Britain would lose a key feature of the Westminster model: producing effective majority parties in Parliament without a majority of votes. The British system would become, at best, rather like the German one where a small, otherwise-irrelevant centrist party generally decides which of the larger parties forms the government. Given that the Liberal Democrats appear ideologically closer to Labour than to the Conservatives, proportional representation would lock the Conservatives in the political wilderness and change British elections for many years to come.

Labour has not embraced proportional representation, however; the party promises to study the issue but a rapid move in favour of this reform is unlikely.[7] In the short term, the sizeable parliamentary majority achieved on under half the vote argues against such a move. Over the longer term, concerns about forcing a permanent coalition on Britain are a strong argument in favour of postponing this particular electoral reform indefinitely. A far more likely challenge to a repeat of history is under the control of the Conservative Party, and again draws parallels to the electoral situation of the first decade of this century.

Free Trade caused deep divisions within the Conservative Party as A. J. Balfour tried to balance demands for trade protection with equally strident demands for an open trading system.[8] Powerful forces pulled the Prime Minister in both directions, and great cunning was needed to avoid a party split. Near-unity was maintained only by convincing leaders of each side that the Prime Minister was truly in favour of both sets of policies. Nevertheless, several people left the party, including Winston Churchill, while others fought within the party but under the Free Trade banner. The similarity with the 1990s is striking: John Major tried to straddle his party's divide between Eurosceptics and others by being all things to all people, but the differences still caused the defection of two MPs in 1996 and led to open rebellion against his leadership during the 1997 election campaign. As of this writing, it is unclear which direction the Conservative Party will take under its new leader, but if the party does split, it will have difficulties similar to those faced by Labour in the 1980s. Such difficulties, and the resulting wilderness stay, are not likely to appeal to members of the Conservative Party.

British history suggests that Labour will not move towards proportional representation, and that the Conservatives will rediscover unity in opposition.[9] In the first instance, political parties rarely vote to reduce their own power; in the second, the Conservatives are well known for their ability to organise themselves in the pursuit of government. We are therefore left with the probability that the general election of 1997, while producing the largest Labour majority in British history and the greatest Conservative humiliation this century, is an aberration. The Conservative Party will most likely return to power within the next three elections. As Labour increasingly responds to the demands of the powerless in the periphery, the more populous core will react more and more vehemently. Liberal action on core–periphery issues in Edwardian Britain doomed the party to defeat. Labour faces the same danger.

## NOTES

1. To be sure, the Conservative decline was less in Wales and Scotland than elsewhere, but then again, the party's vote had so much less far to fall. See especially the forthcoming article by Pippa Norris in *Parliamentary Affairs* 50, 4 (October 1997).
2. The correlation of the distribution of support between 1992 (notional results) and 1997 for the Conservatives and Labour is 0.97 for both parties, while Liberal Democrat support in 1997 correlates at 0.93 with 1992 notional results. Conservative and Labour correlations of 1987 and 1992 are 0.98 and 0.96, respectively. By contrast, support for the Liberal Democrats between 1987 and 1992 was much less stable, with a correlation of 0.84 (see Table 2.3). The 1992 notional results were estimated by Colin Rallings and Michael Thrasher and can be found in C. Rallings and M. Thrasher, *Media Guide to the New Constituencies* (London: BBC/ITN/PANews/Sky, 1995).
3. See Chapter Two above, especially Figure 2.1.
4. R. T. Mackenzie, *British Political Parties: The Distribution of Power within the Conservative and Labour Parties*, 2nd edn (New York: Praeger, 1963), pp. 68–9. A recent analysis can be found in D. A. Irwin, *Against the Tide: An Intellectual History of Free Trade* (Princeton, NJ: Princeton University Press, 1996).
5. C. Seymour, *Electoral Reform in England and Wales: The Development and Operation of the Parliamentary Franchise 1821–1885* (New Haven: Yale University Press, 1915; reprint Hamden, CT: Archon Books, 1970), pp. 305, 335–9.
6. E. S. Wellhofer, *Democracy, Capitalism, and Empire in Late Victoria Britain, 1885–1910* (London: Macmillan, 1996), pp. 39–42, 79–102; R. Waller, *The Almanac of British Politics* (London: Routledge, 1996), pp. xxii–xxv; D. Rossiter, R. J. Johnston and C. J. Pattie, 'Estimating the Partisan Impact of Redistricting in Great Britain', *British Journal of Political Science* 27, 2 (April 1997), pp. 319–31.
7. T. Blair, *New Britain: My Vision of a Young Country* (Boulder: Westview Press, 1996).
8. M. Bentley, *Politics Without Democracy 1815–1914* (London: Fontana Paperbacks, 1984), pp. 307–11.
9. J. Hart, *Proportional Representation: Critics of the British Electoral System 1820–1945* (Oxford: Clarendon Press, 1992); A. Aughey, 'Philosophy and Faction', in P. Norton (ed.), *The Conservative Party* (London: Prentice Hall Harvester Wheatsheaf, 1996), pp. 83–94.

APPENDIX

# Data Sources and Expansions

Data for the dynamic core–periphery model came from a number of sources. This appendix discusses these sources and notes any changes or corrections that were made to bring them into conformity across the entire time span. In addition to the bibliographical reference, a table reports descriptive statistics for each variable.

## AGRICULTURAL RETURNS

- Board of Agriculture, *Agricultural Returns of Great Britain with Abstract Returns for the United Kingdom, British Possessions, and Foreign Countries* (London: HMSO, 1891). Table 2 (pp. 4–31).

- For England and Wales actual data are for 1922. See Ministry of Agriculture and Fisheries, *Agricultural Statistics 1923, Vol. LVII, Part 1, Report on the Acreage Under Crops and Number of Live Stock in England and Wales. With Summary Tables for Great Britain and Ireland* (London: HMSO, 1923). Table 2: 'Acreage under Crops and Grass; and Number of Live Stock; as returned on the 4th June, 1923, and 3rd June, 1922, in each County of England and Wales'. Data on acreage under crops and grass do not include rough grazing land.

- For Scotland actual data are for 1920. See Board of Agriculture for Scotland, *Agriculture Statistics 1920, Vol. IX,*

*e and Live Stock Returns for Scotland*
/ISO, 1921). Table 5: 'Acreage under Crop
number of Horses, Cattle, Sheep, and Pigs,
the 4th of June 1920 in each County of

- For England and Wales: Ministry of Agriculture and Fisheries, *Agricultural Statistics 1950–1. England and Wales. Part 1: Acreage and Production of Crops, and Numbers of Livestock, of Agricultural Workers, of Agricultural Holdings and of Certain Descriptions of Agricultural Machinery* (London: HMSO, 1954). Tables 3–44 (pp. 12–53). Data on crops and grass exclude land devoted to rough grazing.

- For Scotland: Department of Agriculture for Scotland, *Agricultural Statistics 1950 and 1951* (Edinburgh: HMSO, 1953). Tables 2–12 (pp. 12–22) for acreage; Tables 21–31 (pp. 32–42) for sheep population. Data exclude land categorised as 'rough grazing'.

- Ministry of Agriculture, Fisheries, and Food; The Scottish Office Agriculture and Fisheries Department; Department of Agriculture for Northern Ireland; Welsh Office Agriculture Department, *The Digest of Agricultural Census Statistics United Kingdom 1991* (London: HMSO, 1991).


CORPORATE HEADQUARTERS LOCATIONS

- Thomas Skinner (comp.), *The Stock Exchange Yearbook for 1891* (London [n.p.], 1891). To be included companies had to be solvent, publicly traded companies. Railways and municipal services were excluded. Total number of companies: 937.

- Thomas Skinner (comp.), *The Stock Exchange Yearbook for 1921* (London [n.p.], 1921). To be included industrial and commercial companies had to be solvent, publicly traded, and with a minimum capital of £75,000. Total number of companies: 1,344. All companies dealing solely with foreign property or whose headquarters were located in a foreign country were also excluded.

- *The Stock Exchange Official Yearbook for 1952* (London: Thomas Skinner, & Co., 1952). To be included industrial and commercial companies had to be solvent, publicly traded, and with a minimum capital of £725,000. All companies dealing solely with foreign property or whose headquarters were located in a foreign country were also excluded. Total number of companies: 859.

- *The Stock Exchange Official Yearbook 1991–1992* (London: Macmillan, 1992). To be included companies had to be solvent, publicly traded with a minimum capitalization of £5,000,000, with head offices in Britain, and not engaged solely in activities outside Britain. Total number of companies: 1,017.

## POPULATION AND MIGRATION

- 1891 Census of England and Wales; 1891 Census of Scotland.

- 1921 Census of England and Wales; 1921 Census of Scotland. Scottish data for 1921 do not separate population change by migration from change resulting from natural growth. As a result, the 8.15 per cent surplus of births over deaths that was the natural growth rate for England and Wales was extrapolated to Scotland, from which net population change by migration was calculated. Data from counties of Perth to Wigtown are from the preliminary report; the remainder are from the final report. The preliminary and the final report vary in their population data by less than 0.1 per cent. The extraordinary growth rate for Bute (+70 per cent since 1911) is attributed to an unusual number of summer visitors.

- 1951 Census of England and Wales, Table 2; 1951 Census of Scotland. Deaths of non-civilians occurring between 3 September 1939 and 31 December 1949 are not included in net change caused by births and deaths. This serves to inflate returns of population change by migration, as not all deaths are recorded.

- 1991 Census of England and Wales, Table C; 1991 Census of Scotland.


RAILWAYS


Work on the rail network is designed to estimate changes in rail service over time. Counting the number of passenger stations in a county and dividing by the population produces an index of service and a gauge of use. Higher numbers indicate a well-served area whose population is very mobile while lower numbers indicate less mobile populations and worse service. Some distortions occur in areas of high tourist traffic, especially in the time before the widespread use of the car.

Unless otherwise indicated, sources are in the Harvard University Pusey Map collection and described by their assigned call numbers.

- For 1891; England and Wales: 5750 1891Δ. Fifteen sheets with good railways, adequate county boundaries. London (except for the City) is amalgamated with its surrounding counties. Scotland: 5770 1891Δ. 29 sheets, good boundaries and stations.

- For 1921; Britain: 5740 1921Δ. *Bartholomew's Railway Map of the British Isles.* Excellent map. Clear counties, clear stations. Complete and well dated.

- 1957Δ. Ordnance Survey maps of Britain. Copyrights range from 1957 to 1965. For Scotland, 5770 1952Δ, the Scottish Youth Hostels Association, *Touring Map of Scotland* (Edinburgh: John Bartholomew).

- Rand McNally, 1992. *Updated Road Atlas of Britain.* London: Bartholomew.

## ORIGIN OF POLITICAL ÉLITES

Political élites are defined as Members of Parliament in the years under consideration for the first three periods. In 1992 élites include only sitting Members of Parliament who stood for re-election; data on geographic origins for this period were drawn from British Candidate Study, 1992, which was directed by Professor Joni Lovenduski (Southampton University) and Dr Pippa Norris (Harvard University). The study was funded by the Economic and Social Research Council (R000-23-1991). This author is grateful for access.

For other elections, biographies of MPs were examined for references to birthplace. *Dod's Parliamentary Companion* and *Who's Who* were both examined for 1892, 1923, and 1952. When no birthplace was cited, origin was assigned according to the following criteria, in descending order of preference; 1. birthplaces mentioned in other editions of *Who's Who*: 2. birthplace taken from the *Dictionary of National Biography* or *The Complete Peerage*; 3. parental residence (from *Who's Who*) at year of MP's birth; 4. place of primary education, when such was not a boarding school; 5. reference to paternal origins; 6. occupation, when such consisted of collier or trade unionist.

The following works were examined:
*Dod's Parliamentary Companion*, for 1892, 1923, and 1952.
*Who's Who*, for 1910, 1919, 1947, 1952, and 1953.
*The Dictionary of National Biography* for 1921–30, 1931–40, 1951–60, 1961–70, 1971–80, and 1981–85.
*The Complete Peerage of England, Scotland, Ireland, Great Britain and the United Kingdom* (1916).

## NEWSPAPER PUBLISHING

One indicator of cultural power is the degree of local control over news sources. Data on the number of newspaper titles that appear in each county are an indicator of this. Data were drawn for 1899, 1921, 1951, and 1992 from *Willings Press Guide* and its antecedents.

## CONSTRUCTING THE CORE–PERIPHERY MODELS

Chapter Five discussed the creation of one core–periphery supervariable from the 1891 data and two supervariables from the data for the other years. This section of the appendix provides the statistical explanation for this.

Performing a factor analysis on the variables for each model suggested a one-factor solution for 1891 and two-factor solutions for 1921, 1951, and 1991. The eigenvalues of these analyses are presented in Table A1.

TABLE A1
EIGENVALUES FOR PRINCIPLE COMPONENTS EXTRACTION ON
CORE–PERIPHERY VARIABLES

| Number of factors | 1891 | 1921 | 1951 | 1991 |
|---|---|---|---|---|
| 1 | 3.37 | 3.25 | 3.36 | 1.85 |
| 2 | 1.08 | 1.20 | 1.35 | 1.23 |
| 3 | 0.75 | 0.77 | 0.58 | 1.04 |
| 4 | 0.51 | 0.43 | 0.42 | 0.76 |
| 5 | 0.25 | 0.29 | 0.19 | 0.69 |
| 6 | 0.05 | 0.07 | 0.10 | 0.43 |

Source: See text.

Factor one, on to which the head office, MP origin, newspaper title, and railway variables are positively loaded, relates to the degree of 'connectedness' that a county has with the core. Factor two, on to which the migration variable loaded negatively and the sheep density variable loaded positively, relates to the 'marginalisation of the county'. These supervariables are further explained in Chapter Five.

# Bibliography

P. N. Balchin, *Regional Policy in Britain: The North-South Divide* (London: Paul Chapman, 1990).

F. Barth, *Ethnic Groups and Boundaries: The Social Organization of Cultural Difference* (Boston: Little, Brown, 1969).

S. Bartolini and P. Mair, *Identity, Competition and Electoral Availability: The Stabilisation of European Electorates 1885–1985* (Cambridge: Cambridge University Press, 1990).

D. E. D. Beales, *The Political Parties of Nineteenth Century Britain* (London: Historical Association, 1971).

S. Beer, *Modern British Politics: Parties and Pressure Groups in the Collectivist Age* (New York: W. W. Norton, 1982).

M. Bentley, *Politics Without Democracy: Perception and Preoccupation in British Government* (London: Fontana, 1984).

N. Blewett, *The Peers the Parties, and the People* (London: Macmillan, 1972).

V. Bogdanor, 'Electoral Pacts in Britain Since 1886', in D. Kavanagh (ed.), *Electoral Politics* (Oxford: Clarendon Press, 1992).

V. Bogdanor and W. H. Field, 'Lessons of History: Core and Periphery in British Electoral Behaviour, 1910–1992', *Electoral Studies*, 12, 3 (September 1993) pp. 204–24.

H. N. Brailsford, *The War of Steel and Gold* (London: G. Bell & Sons Ltd, 1914).

T. Brown, *Migration and Politics* (Chapel Hill, NC: University of North Carolina Press, 1988).

D. Butler, A. Adonis, and T. Travers, *Failure in British Government: The Politics of the Poll Tax* (Oxford: Oxford University Press, 1994).

D. Butler and D. Kavanagh, *The British General Election of 1992* (London: Macmillan, 1992).

D. E. Butler and D. Stokes, *Political Change in Britain* (London: Macmillan, 1969).

D. E. Butler and D. Stokes, *Political Change in Britain*, 2nd. edition (London: Macmillan, 1974).

H. D. Clarke and M. C. Stewart, 'Economic Evaluations and Electoral Outcomes: An Evaluation of Alternative Forecasting Models', in Broughton, *et al.* (eds), *British Elections and Parties Yearbook 1994* (London: Frank Cass, 1995).

P. F. Clarke, *Lancashire and the New Liberalism* (Cambridge: Cambridge University Press, 1971).

H. F. L. Cocks, *The Nonconformist Conscience* (London: Independent Press, 1943).

C. Cook, *A Short History of the Liberal Party* (New York: St. Martin's Press, 1976).

P. J. Corfield, *The Impact of English Towns 1700-1800* (Oxford: Oxford University Press, 1982).

G. W. Cox, *The Efficient Secret: the Cabinet and the Development of Political Parties in Victorian England* (Cambridge: Cambridge University Press, 1987).

I. Crewe, P. Norris, and R. Waller, 'The 1992 General Election', in I. Crewe, P. Norris, D. Denver, and D. Broughton (eds), *British Elections and Parties Yearbook: 1992* (London: Harvester Wheatsheaf, 1992).

R. E. Crum and G. Gudgin, *Non-Production Activities in UK Manufacturing Industry* (Brussels: Commission of the European Community, 1977).

J. Curtice, 'One Nation?', in R. Jowell, S. Witherspoon, and L. Brook (eds), *British Social Attitudes: The Fifth Report* (Aldershot: Gower, 1988).

J. Curtice and M. Steed, 'Electoral Choice and the Production of Government: The Changing Operation of the Electoral System in the United Kingdom Since 1955', *British Journal of Political Science*, 12, 3 (July 1982) pp. 249–98.

J. Curtice and M. Steed, 'Proportionality and Exaggeration in the British Electoral System', *Electoral Studies* 5, 3 (December 1986) pp. 209–28.

J. Curtice and M. Steed, 'The Results Analysed', in D. Butler and D. Kavanagh (eds), *The British General Election of 1987* (New York: St. Martin's Press, 1988).

R. J. Dalton, *Citizen Politics in Western Democracies: Public Opinion and Political Parties in the United States, Great Britain, West Germany, and France* (Chatham, NJ: Chatham House, 1988).

R. J. Dalton, S. C. Flanagan, and P. A. Beck (eds), *Electoral Change in Advanced Industrial Democracies: Realignment or Dealignment?* (Princeton: Princeton University Press, 1984).

D. Denver and K. Halfacree, 'Inter-Constituency Migration and Party Support in Britain', *Political Studies*, 40, 3 (September 1992) pp. 571–80.

K. Deutsch, *Nationalism and Social Communication* (Cambridge, MA: MIT Press, 1955).

K. Deutsch, 'Social Mobilization and Political Development', *American Political Science Review*, 55, 4 (December 1961) pp. 494–513.

M. Eagles, 'An Ecological Perspective on Working-Class Political Behaviour', in R. J. Johnston, F. Shelley, and P. Taylor (eds), *Developments in Electoral Geography* (London: Routledge, 1990).

W. H. Field, 'Council House Sales and Local Governments: A Case of Conflicting Goals', *Representation*, forthcoming.

W. H. Field, 'Council Housing and the Expansion of a Conservative Electorate: Some Aggregate Results and their Causes', paper presented at the Annual Meeting of the Political Studies Association Specialist Group on Elections, Public Opinion and Parties, Great Northern Hotel, London, 15–17 September 1995.

W. H. Field, 'Electoral Volatility and the Structure of Competition: A Reassessment of Voting Patterns in Britain 1959-92', *West European Politics*, 17, 4 (October 1994) pp. 149–65.

A. G. Frank, *Crisis: In the Third World* (New York: Holmes and Meier Publishers, 1981).

J. Galtung, 'A Structural Theory of Imperialism', *Journal of Peace Research*, 8 (1971).

P. L. Garside, 'London and the Home Counties', in F. M. L. Thompson (ed.), *The Cambridge Social History of Britain 1750–1950. Volume 1: Regions and Communities* (Cambridge: Cambridge University Press, 1990).

N. Gash, *Politics in the Age of Peel,* 2nd ed. (Hassocks: Harvester, 1977).

M. D. George, *London Life in the Eighteenth Century* (Chicago: Academy Chicago, 1984).

W. E. Gladstone, *A Chapter of Autobiography,* 2nd ed. (London, 1868).

W. E. Gladstone, 'The County Franchise and Mr. Lowe Thereon', *Nineteenth Century,* 2 (November 1877).

J. F. Glaser, 'English Nonconformity and the Decline of Liberalism', *American Historical Review,* 63, 2 (January 1958) pp. 352–63.

C. A. E. Goodhart, and R. J. Bhansali, 'Political Economy', *Political Studies,* 18, 1 (March 1970) pp. 43–106.

P. A. Hall, *Governing the Economy: The Politics of State Intervention in*

*Britain and France* (New York: Oxford University Press, 1986).

H. J. Hanham, *Elections and Party Management: Politics in the Time of Disraeli and Gladstone* (London: Longman, 1959).

M. Harrop, A. Heath, and S. Openshaw, 'Does Neighborhood Influence Voting Behaviour – and Why?' in I. Crewe, P. Norris, D. Denver, and D. Broughton (eds), *British Elections and Parties Yearbook: 1991* (London: Harvester Wheatsheaf, 1992).

M. J. Healey and H. D. Watts, 'The Multi-Plant Enterprise', in W. F. Lever (ed.), *Industrial Change in the United Kingdom* (London: Longman, 1987).

A. Heath, R. Jowell, and J. Curtice, 'Can Labour Win?' in A. Heath, R. Jowell, and John Curtice, with Bridget Taylor (eds), *Labour's Last Chance? The 1992 Election and Beyond* (Aldershot: Dartmouth, 1994).

A. F. Heath, R. Jowell, J. Curtice, G. Evans, J. Field, and S. Witherspoon, *Understanding Political Change: The British Voter, 1964–1987* (Oxford: Pergamon Press: 1991).

M. Hechter, *Internal Colonialism: The Celtic Fringe in British National Development 1536–1966* (Berkeley and Los Angeles: University of California Press, 1975).

H. T. Himmelweit, P. Humphreys, and M. Jaeger, *How Voters Decide*, revised ed. (Milton Keynes: Open University, 1985).

A. O. Hirschman, *Exit, Voice, and Loyalty; Responses to Decline in Firms, Organizations, and States* (Cambridge: Harvard University Press, 1970).

J. A. Hobson, 'The General Election: A Sociological Interpretation', *The Sociological Review,* 32 (April 1910) pp. 105–17.

S. Holmberg, 'Party Identification Compared Across the Atlantic', in M. K. Jennings and T. E. Mann (eds), *Elections at Home and Abroad: Essays in Honor of Warren E. Miller* (Ann Arbor: University of Michigan Press, 1994).

M. Howard, *War and the Liberal Conscience.* updated edition (Oxford: Oxford University Press, 1989).

C. T. Husbands, *Racial Exclusionism and the City* (London: Allen and Unwin, 1983).

R. Inglehart, *Culture Shift in Advanced Industrial Society* (Princeton: Princeton University Press, 1990).

D. A. Irwin, 'Industry or Class Cleavages over Trade Policy? Evidence from the British General Election of 1923', National Bureau of Economic Research, Inc., Working Paper No. 5170, 1995.

D. A. Irwin, 'The Politics of Free Trade: Voting in the British General Election of 1906', *Journal of Law and Economics*, 37, 1 (April 1994) pp. 75–108.

R. J. Johnston, A. B. O'Neill, and P. J. Taylor, 'The Geography of Party Support: Comparative Studies in Electoral Stability', in Manfred J. Holler (ed.), *The Logic of Multiparty Systems* (Dordrecht: Kluwer Academic Publishers, 1987).

R. J. Johnston and C. J. Pattie, 'Voting in Britain: A Growing North–South Divide?' in J. Lewis and A. Townsend (eds), *The North–South Divide: Regional Change in Britain in the 1980s* (London: Paul Chapman, 1989).

R. J. Johnston, C. J. Pattie, and J. G. Allsop, *A Nation Dividing? The Electoral Map of Great Britain, 1979–87* (London: Longman, 1988).

K. Jones, R. J. Johnston, and C. J. Pattie, 'People, Places, and Regions: Exploring the Use of Multi-Level Modeling in the Analysis of Electoral Data', *British Journal of Political Science*, 22, 3 (July 1992) pp. 343–80.

S. Kendrick and D. McCrone, 'Politics in a Cold Climate: The Conservative Decline in Scotland', *Political Studies*, 37, 4 (December 1989) pp. 589–603.

S. Kuhnle, P. Flora, and D. Urwin, *State Formation, National-Building, and Mass Politics in Europe: The Theory of Stein Rokkan* (Oxford: Oxford University Press, 1996).

C. H. Lee, 'Regional Growth and Structural Change in Victorian Britain', *Economic History Review*, 34, 3 (1981) pp. 438–52.

J. Lewis and A. Townsend, *The North–South Divide: Regional Change in Britain in the 1980s* (London: Paul Chapman, 1989).

A. Leyshon and N. Thrift. 'South Goes North? The Rise of the British Provincial Financial Centre', in J. Lewis and A. Townsend (eds), *The North–South Divide: Regional Change in Britain in the 1980s* (London: Paul Chapman, 1989).

A. Lijphart, *Electoral Systems and Party Systems: A Study of Twenty-Seven Democracies, 1945–1990* (Oxford: Oxford University Press, 1994).

S. M. Lipset and S. Rokkan, 'Cleavage Structures, Party Systems, and Voter Alignments: An Introduction', in S. M. Lipset and S. Rokkan (eds), *Party Systems and Voter Alignments* (New York: The Free Press, 1967).

I. McAllister and D. T. Studlar, 'Region and Voting in Britain 1979–87: Territorial Polarization or Artifact?', *American Journal of Political Science*, 36, 1 (February 1992), pp. 168–99.

R. McKibbin, 'Class and the Conventional Wisdom: The Conservative

Party and the "Public" in Inter-war Britain', in R. McKibbin, *The Ideologies of Class: Social Relations in Britain 1880–1950* (Oxford: Oxford University Press, 1991).

D. McMahon, A. F. Heath, M. Harrop, and J. Curtice, 'The Electoral Consequences of North–South Migration', *British Journal of Political Science*, 22, 4 (October 1992) pp. 419–44.

M. Maguire, 'Is There Still Persistence: Electoral Change in Western Europe, 1948–1979', in H. Daalder and P. Mair (eds), *Western European Party Systems: Continuity and Change* (London: Sage, 1979).

A. Marr, *The Battle for Scotland* (London: Penguin Books, 1992).

D. Marsh, H. Ward, D. Sanders, and S. Price, 'Modelling Government Popularity in Britain, 1979–87: A Disaggregated Approach', in I. Crewe, P. Norris, D. Denver, and D. Broughton (eds), *British Elections and Parties Yearbook: 1991* (London: Harvester Wheatsheaf, 1992).

R. Martin, 'The Political Economy of Britain's North–South Divide', in J. Lewis and A. Townsend (eds), *The North–South Divide: Regional Change in Britain in the 1980s* (London: Paul Chapman, 1989).

C. Matthew, R. McKibbin, and J. Kay, 'The Franchise Factor in the Rise of the Labour Party', *English Historical Review*, 91, 361 (October 1976) pp. 723–52.

R. Melson and H. Wolpe, 'Modernization and the Politics of Communication: A Theoretical Perspective', *American Political Science Review*, 64, 4 (December 1970) pp. 1112–30.

W. L. Miller, *Electoral Dynamics in Britain Since 1918* (London: Macmillan, 1977).

W. L. Miller, *The End of British Politics? Scots and English Political Behaviour in the Seventies* (Oxford: Clarendon Press, 1981).

W. L. Miller, 'The De-Nationalisation of British Politics: The Re-Emergence of the Periphery', *West European Politics*, 6, 4 (October 1983) pp. 103–29.

J. Mitchell and L. G. Bennie, 'Thatcherism and the Scottish Question', in C. Rallings, D. M. Farrell, D. Denver, and D. Broughton (eds), *British Elections and Parties Yearbook: 1995* (London: Frank Cass, 1996).

B. Moore, J. Rhodes, and P. Tyler, *The Impact of Regional Policy on Regional Labour Markets* (Cambridge: Department of Applied Economics, Cambridge University, 1981).

K. O. Morgan, *David Lloyd George 1863–1945* (Cardiff: University of Wales Press, 1981).

K. O. Morgan, *Wales in British Politics 1868–1922* (Cardiff: University of Wales Press, 1970).

T. Nairn, *The Break-Up of Britain* (London: NLB, 1977).

H. Norpoth, *Confidence Regained: Economics, Mrs. Thatcher, and the British Voter* (Ann Arbor: University of Michigan Press, 1992).

M. Ostrogorski, *Democracy and the Organisation of Political Parties*, reprinted 1970 (London: Haskell House, 1902).

J. R. Owens, and L. L. Wade. 'Economic Conditions and Constituency Voting in Great Britain', *Political Studies*, 36, 1 (January 1988) pp. 30–51.

Charles Stuart Parker (ed.), *Sir Robert Peel. From his Private Papers* (London: John Murray, 1891–99).

C. Pattie, E. Fieldhouse, R. Johnston, and A. Russell, 'A Widening Regional Cleavage in British Voting Behaviour: Some Preliminary Explorations', in I. Crewe, P. Norris, D. Denver, and D. Broughton (eds), *British Elections and Parties Yearbook: 1991* (London: Harvester Wheatsheaf, 1992).

B. Paulson, 'The Economy and the 1992 Election: Was 1992 Labour's Golden Chance?', in A. Heath, R. Jowell, and J. Curtice, with B. Taylor (eds), *Labour's Last Chance? The 1992 Election and Beyond* (Aldershot: Dartmouth, 1994).

H. Perkin, *The Origin of Modern British Society, 1780–1880* (London: Routledge & Kegan Paul, 1969).

F. F. Piven (ed.), *Labour Parties in Post-industrial Societies* (Oxford: Polity Press, 1991).

M. Pugh, *The Making of Modern British Politics*, 2nd ed. (Oxford: Blackwell, 1993).

S. Rokkan, 'Nation Building, Cleavage Formation, and the Structuring of Mass Politics', in S. Rokkan (ed.), *Citizens, Elections, Parties* (Oslo: Universitetsforlaget, 1970).

S. Rokkan and D. Urwin, *The Politics of Territorial Identity: Studies in European Regionalism* (Beverly Hills, CA: Sage, 1982).

R. Rose, 'From Simple Determinism to Interactive Models of Voting: Britain as an Example', *Comparative Political Studies*, 15, 2 (July 1982) pp. 145–70.

W. D. Rubenstein, 'British Millionaires, 1809–1949', *Bulletin of the Institute of Historical Research*, 47, 116 (November 1974) pp. 202–23.

W. D. Rubenstein, 'Victorian Middle Classes: Wealth, Occupation, and Geography', *Economic History Review*, 30, 4 (1977), pp. 602-23.

W. D. Rubenstein, 'Wealth, Elites, and the Class Structure of Modern Britain', *Past and Present*, 76 (August 1977) pp. 99–126.

D. Sanders, 'Economic Performance, Management Competence, and the Outcome of the Next General Election', *Political Studies*, 44, 2 (June 1996) pp. 203–31.

D. Sanders and S. Price, 'Party Support and Economic Perceptions in the UK 1979–87: A Two-Level Approach', in D. Broughton, *et al.* (eds), *British Elections and Parties Yearbook: 1994* (London: Frank Cass, 1995).

Y. Saueressig-Schreuder, 'The Impact of British Colonial Rule on the Urban Hierarchy of Burma', *Review*, 2 (Fall, 1986) pp. 245–77.

C. S. Seymour, *Electoral Reform in England and Wales: The Development of the Parliamentary Franchise 1832–1885* (New Haven: Yale University Press, 1915).

M. Shamir, 'Are Western European Party Systems "Frozen"?', *Comparative Political Studies*, 17, 1 (April 1984) pp. 35–79.

E. R. A. N. Smith, *The Unchanging American Voter* (Berkeley and Los Angeles: University of California Press, 1989).

M. Steed, 'The Core–Periphery Dimension of British Politics', *Political Geography Quarterly*, 5 (1986), pp. S91–103.

J. Stevenson, *Third Party Politics Since 1945: Liberals, Alliance and Liberal Democrats* (Oxford: Blackwell, 1993).

D. Tanner, *Political Change and the Labour Party 1900–1918* (Cambridge: Cambridge University Press, 1990).

F. M. L. Thompson, *The Cambridge Social History of Britain 1750–1950* (Cambridge: Cambridge University Press, 1990).

F. M. L. Thompson, 'Town and City', in F. M. L. Thompson (ed.), *The Cambridge Social History of Britain 1750–1950. Volume I: Regions and Communities* (Cambridge: Cambridge University Press, 1990).

N. Thrift, A. Leyshon, and P. Daniels, *Sexy Greedy: The New International Financial System, the City of London, and the Southeast of England* (University of Bristol and University of Liverpool: Working Papers on Producer Services No. 8, 1987).

E. A. Tiryakian and R. Rogowski, *New Nationalisms of the Developed West: Toward Explanation* (Boston: Allen and Unwin, 1985).

E. Tufte, *Political Control of the Economy* (Princeton: Princeton University Press, 1978).

D. Urwin, 'The Price of a Kingdom: Territory, Identity and the Centre–Periphery Dimension in Western Europe', in Y. Mény and V. Wright (eds), *Centre–Periphery Relations in Western Europe* (London: Allen and Unwin, 1985).

D. Urwin, 'Toward the Nationalization of British Politics?', in Otto

Büsch (ed.), *Wählerbewegungen in der Europäischen Geschichte* (Berlin: Colloquium Verlag, 1980).

K. Wald, *Crosses on the Ballot: Patterns of British Voter Alignment Since 1885* (Princeton: Princeton University Press, 1983).

W. Wallace, 'Survival and Revival,' in V. Bogdanor (ed.), *Liberal Party Politics* (Oxford: Clarendon Press, 1983).

I. Wallerstein, *Historical Capitalism* (New York: NLB, 1983).

H. D. Watts, 'Non-financial Head Offices: A View from the North', in J. Lewis and A. Townsend (eds), *The North–South Divide: Regional Change in Britain in the 1980s* (London: Paul Chapman, 1989).

E. S. Wellhofer, 'Core and Periphery: Territorial Dimensions in Politics', *Urban Studies*, 26 (1989) pp. 340–55.

E. S. Wellhofer, *Democracy, Capitalism and Empire in Late Victorian Britain* (London: Macmillan, 1996).

E. S. Wellhofer, 'Models of Core and Periphery Dynamics', *Comparative Political Studies*, 21, 2 (July 1988) pp. 281–307.

E. A Wrigley, 'A Simple Model of London's Importance in Changing English Society and Economy 1650-1750', *Past and Present*, 37 (July 1967), pp. 44–70.

# Index

Aberdeen, 122
Adonis, Andrew, 46
Agricultural Returns, 109
Alford index, 55
Allsop, J. G., 2, 64, 74
Ambler, John, 8
Anglican Church, 43, 166–7 and
    core–periphery placement, 86–7
    political differences with
        Nonconformist groups, 32
    political influence, 12
Argyll, 29, 115
Asquith, Herbert, 36, 38, 39–40, 129
Attlee, Clement, 49

Bagehot, Walter, 28
Balchin, Peter, 94
Ballot Act (1872), 18
Barth, Raymond, 148
Bartolini, Stefano, 4, 11, 16
Beales, D. E. D., 28
Beck, Paul Allen, 4
Bedfordshire, 115, 122
Bennie, Lynn, 46
Bentley, Michael, 93
Berkshire, 141
Bhansali, R. J., 73
Birrell, Augustine, 129
*Blackwood's Magazine*, 36
Blair, Tony, 176, 178
Blewett, Neil, 3, 16, 32, 36, 37
Bogdanor, Vernon, 3, 48, 51
Bonar Law, Andrew, 39
Boundary Commission of England,
    141
Brailsford, H. N., 38
British Candidate Study, 134
British Empire Party, 175
Brougham, Lord, 71
Brown, Thad, 70
Buckinghamshire, 141

Burnham, Walter, 50
Butler, David, 2, 6, 16, 46, 65, 66, 84
Butskellism, 44–5, 163

Caernarfon, 30
Cardiff, 128
Catholic Church, 10, 33
    and religious emancipation, 17
Chamberlain, Joseph, 33, 37
Chartists, 29
Cheshire, 89
Churchill, Winston, 129
Clarke, Harold, 5
Cleavage systems and power
    structures, 101
Cleveland, 128
Cocks, H. F. L., 12
Communist International and Labour
    Party, 95
Communist Party of Great Britain, 39
Connectedness as core–periphery
    measure, 153
Conservative Party,
    and Anglicanism, 32, 159–60, 169
    and core–periphery cleavage, 92–4
    and Corn Laws debates, 175
    and Free Trade, 40, 48
    and future policy, 177–8
    and Ireland, 32
    and regional support, 158–63
    and Scotland, 11
    and Wales, 12
    electoral activity (1914–18), 39
    electoral support, by region, 31–2,
        33, 34
    electoral support, by region
        (1885–1910), 38
    electoral support, by region
        (1918–35), 36–7
    electoral support, by region
        (1945–92), 44–7

electoral support (1951), 116
electoral support and economic
   performance (twentieth century),
   74
ideological base, 48
origins of, 12, 92
Consumer's England, 89
Core–periphery cleavage
   and agricultural practices, 108–16
   and party system effects, 172–6
   and political parties, 96–7
   as dynamic model, 90, 100–4,
    169–70
   construction of dynamic model,
    152–8
   defined, 82
   economic aspects of, 107–23
   impact of nationalisation of
    industry, 117
   geography of (1910), 89
   geography of (1955–92), 50–7
   geography of dynamic model,
    169–70
   neo-Liberal model, 82
   neo-Marxian model, 83
   static nature of model, 79, 83–90
   testing of dynamic model, 158–63
   utility of dynamic model, 169–70
Corfield, Peter, 85
Corn Laws repeal (1846), 10, 32, 175
Cornwall, 89, 115, 122, 150
Corporate head office density as
   core–periphery indicator, 116–23
Corporation Act (repeal of), 13
Corrupt Practices Act (1883), 28
Cox, Gary, 18
Crewe, Ivor, 166
Crofters' Party, 35
Crum, R. E., 116
Cumbria, 128
Curtice, John, 2, 17, 45, 52, 64, 67,
   70–1, 73
Cymru Fydd, 35

Dalton, Russell, 4, 74
Daniels, P., 141
Denver, David, 70
Deutsch, Karl, 82
Devolution, 3, 14, 177–8
Devon, 89, 122
Disraeli, Benjamin, 18, 175
Drax, J. W. E. Erle, 29

Durham, 128

Eagles, Munroe, 66
East Anglia, 89
Economic structure, 66
   France, 177
   Italy, 177
Edinburgh, 122, 128, 149
Electoral behaviour
   institutional model, 4
   rational model, 5–6, 65, 71–5
   social identity model, 4, 6, 64–71,
    78–80
   Social psychology model, *see*
    *Electoral behaviour, social identity*
    *model*
Electoral choice
   and concentration effect, 66
   and social identity model, 79–80
   and economic conditions, 72–5
   influences on, 65–6
Electoral cleavages
   and urban–rural divide, 45
   electoral pacts, 43
   ethno-national differences, 87
   in France, 13
   in Germany, 13
   north–south divide, 46
   *See also* Social cleavages
Essex, 115, 141
Essex Man, 2, 80–1
European Union, 48, 173–4
   and Conservative Party, 175
   and Labour Party, 95
Evans, Geoff, 2, 67

Falkland (Malvinas) Islands, 93
Field, Julia, 2, 67
Field, William, 3, 4, 16, 48, 51, 52, 71,
   177
Fieldhouse, E., 1, 2
First World War
   electoral effects of, 38–40, 41
Flanagan, Scott, 4
Flora, Peter, 78
Foot, Michael, 45, 69
France
   and church–state cleavage, 8
   and local government reform, 178
   and social cleavages, 9
   franchise, 10, 13
   expansion of (1918), 41

male, 19
female, 34
Franchise Act (1884), 28
Frank, Andre Gunder, 83
Free Trade, 40, 43, 48

Galtung, Johann, 103, 148, 179
Garside, P. L., 85, 115, 140
Gash, Neil, 29
General Agreement of Tariffs and
    Trade (GATT), 9–10
General election (1886), 34
General election (1900), 93
General election (1906), 36, 50
General election (January 1910), 36–7,
    100, 116, 159
General election (1918), 40, 44
General election (1922), 40, 41–2, 100,
    159–60
General election (1923), 40
General election (1931), 43
General election (1935), 40
General election (1945), 50
General election (1950), 102
General election (1951), 116, 160–3
General election (1955), 1
General election (1964), 43
General election (1987), 81, 102
General election (1992), 79–81, 89, 100,
    161–3
General elections
    and electoral stability, 50
    and electoral volatility, 4
    and national swing, 11
    and party support (1832–85), 31–2
    and uncontested seats, 31
    and uniform swing, 45
    Westminster model of, 44
George, M. D., 86
Germany
    and First World War, 38
    and social cleavages, 9, 13
Gilbert, W. S., 4
Gladstone, William E., 12, 31, 33, 36
Glamorgan, 122, 149
Glasgow, 122, 149
Gloucester, 122, 128
Goodhart, C. A. E., 73
Government policy
    Keynesianism, 93
    regional aid, 93–4, 177
Grey, Edward (Grey of Falloden), 38

Grimond, Jo, 57, 176
Gudgin G., 116

Halfacree, Keith, 70
Hall, Peter, 175
Hanham, H. J., 18–19, 28, 29
Harrop, Martin, 17, 66, 70–1
Healey, M. J., 117
Heath, Anthony, 2, 16, 17, 66, 67,
    70–1, 84
Hechter, Michael, 64, 79, 88, 179
Hertfordshire, 115
Highland Land League, 35
Himmelweit, Hilda, 16
Hirshman, A. O., 103
Hobson, J. A., 3, 37, 89
Holmberg, Soeren, 4
Holyoake, G. J., 30
House of Lords, reform of, 34, 36, 167
Hull, 122
Humphreys, Patrick, 16
Husbands, Christopher, 66

India, 93
Inglehart, Ronald, 16
Internal trade, 135
Inverness, 115
Ireland
    and Disestablishment, 13
    and Liberal Party election victories,
        31, 172–3
    and Repeal agitation, 13
    Home Rule for, 18, 33, 93, 167, 172
    independence for, 42
    Nationalist Party support, 33, 34,
        172–3
Irwin, Douglas, 140
Italy, 8

Jaeger, Marianne, 16
Jenkins, Roy, 45
Johnston, Ron, 1, 2, 5, 17, 64, 72
Jones, K., 2, 5
Jowell, Roger, 2, 67

Kavanagh, Dennis, 2
Kay, John, 12, 19, 41
Kendrick, Stephen, 64
Kent, 115, 129, 149, 151
Keynes, John Maynard, 39, 42
Kinnock, Neil, 69
Kuhnle, Stein, 78

Labour Party
  and class cleavage, 44
  and core–periphery cleavage, 92,
    95–6, 172–3
  and devolution for Scotland, 175–6
  and future policy options, 178
  and London, 96
  and Popular Front, 39
  and the Liberal government (1910),
    34
  electoral activity (1914–18), 39
  electoral results (1955–92), 45–7
  electoral support, Scotland, 11
  electoral support, Wales, 12
  origins of, 43, 49, 57, 92, 95
  party split (1981), 45
  regional electoral support, 44, 57
Lancashire, 89, 149
Lee, C. H., 86
Lewis, James, 177
Leyshon, A., 141
Liberal Party
  alliance with Conservatives, 44, 49
  alliance with Social Democratic
    Party, 45
  and core–periphery cleavage, 42–3,
    92, 94–5
  and political devolution, 95, 174,
    176
  and Free Trade, 48
  and Home Rule, 35
  and Ireland, 31, 95, 172–3
  and nuclear disarmament, 95
  and Popular Front, 39
  and religious demands, 13, 43
  and Scottish nationalism, 36
  and social cleavages, 46
  collapse of, 38–43, 172
  electoral activity (1914–18), 39
  electoral support, 31–2, 36–7
  electoral support, by region
    (1885–1910), 34–8
  electoral support, by region
    (1918–35), 38–43
  electoral support, by region
    (1945–92), 44–7
  electoral support, nineteenth
    century, 31, 33
  electoral support, Scotland, 11, 31, 40
  electoral support, Wales, 12, 31
  ideological base, 49
  internal party structure, 46

  origins of, 12, 32, 92
  split (1886), 33, 50
  split (1918–35), 40
  regional electoral support, 55, 178
  religious base, 32–3, 166–7
Liberal Unionist Party
  alliance with Conservative Party, 93
  electoral support, by region
    (1885–1910), 50
  origins of, 33
Lijphart, Arend, 176
Lipset, Seymour Martin, 7
Lloyd George, David, 30, 35, 39–41, 49
Local government, 49
  and the north–south divide, 177–8
London, 115, 122–3, 128, 140, 141, 149,
    150, 151
  and core–periphery placement,
    85–7, 171
  social problems, 86
Lothian, 115
Lovenduski, Joni, 134
Lowell, A. Lawrence, 18

McAllister, Ian, 2, 64, 67–70, 162
Macaulay, Thomas Babbington
    (Lord), 12, 93, 169
McCrone, David, 64
McKibbin, Ross, 12, 19, 41
Mackinder, H. J., 86
McMahon, Dorren, 17, 70–1
Maguire, Maria, 11
Mair, Peter, 4, 11, 16
Marginalisation, as core–periphery
    measure, 153–8
Marr, Andrew, 35, 44
Marriage Act (1836), 32
Marsh, David, 74
Martin, R., 2
Mary, Queen of Scots, 12
Matthew, Colin, 12, 19, 41
Members of Parliament, as
    core–periphery indicator, 128–35
Merthyr Tydfil, 30
Middlesex, 115
Migration, 70–1
  as core–periphery indicator, 140–50
Miller, William, 11, 34, 36, 49, 64, 78,
    89, 104, 117, 161
Milton Keynes, 141
Mitchell, James, 46
Mond, Sir Alfred, 43

Moray, 122
Morgan, K. O., 35

Nairn, Tom, 83
Newcastle, 128, 149
Newspaper distribution, as core–
    periphery indicator, 123–9
Nonconformism
    and religious emancipation, 17
    political influence, 12, 32–3, 166–7
Norpoth, Helmut, 74
Norris, Pippa, 134, 166
North Yorkshire, 141
North–south divide, 6, 16–17
    and social change, 66–71
    defined, 27
    explanations for, 64–5
    growth of, 55
    similarity, 1992 to 1910, 166–7

Occupations, distribution of
    (1951–91), 67
Openshaw, Stan, 66
Ostrogorski, M., 31
Owen, David, 45
Owens, John R., 5, 73, 102
Oxfordshire, 141

Parker, Charles Stuart, 12
Parkes, Joseph, 29
Parliamentary divisions, 18
Partisan alignment, 50–3
Pattie, Charles, 1, 2, 5, 17, 64, 74
Paulson, Bruno, 5
Peel, Sir Robert, 13, 32, 175
Perkin, H., 32
Piven, F. F., 4
Plaid Cymru, 35, 55, 175
Political issues, regional dimension to,
    33–4, 36, 176–7
Poll Tax, 46
Population growth, 140
Population migration, 70–1, 140–2
Price, Simon, 5, 74
Producer's England, 89
Pugh, Martin, 30

Raab, Gillian, 36
Railway service, 86, 148–52
Redistribution Act (1885), 28
Reform Act (1867), 17, 29, 31
Reform Acts (1883–84), 17–19, 28, 57

Regional cleavages
    and attitudes toward London, 84–5
    and class distribution, 75
    and economic conditions, 72–5
    and leader effects, 69
    and migration, 70–1
Regional aid, 93–4, 177
Registration Act (1885), 28
Religion and Politics, 3, 12, 33, 43,
    159–60, 166–7
Richard, Henry, 30
Rodgers, William, 45
Rogowski, R., 78
Rokkan, Stein, 7–11, 34, 167
Rose, Richard, 15, 89, 162
Ross and Cromarty, 115
Rotten boroughs, 29
Rubenstein, W. D., 2
Russell, Andrew, 1, 2
Rutland, 115

Sanders, David, 5, 74
Saueressig–Shreuder, Yda, 143
Scotland
    and core–periphery placement, 87–9
    and devolution, 81
    and Liberal Party, 40
    devolution of power to, 174
    Home Rule for, 35
    independence for, 174–5
    nationalism, 84
    Scottish Assembly, 173
    Scottish Convention, 44
Scottish National Party (SNP), 2, 36,
    54, 79
    and Scottish devolution, 174, 176
    electoral results (1945), 44
Scottish Office, 88, 177
Seymour, Charles, 28, 29, 30
Shamir, Michal, 11
Sheep farming, as core–periphery
    indicator, 109–16
Simon, Sir John, 40, 42
Smith, Eric R. A. N., 4
Social cleavages, 7–10
    and Liberal Party decline, 42–3
    church–state, 8
    core–periphery, 9, 11, 14–15, 17,
    42–3
    class, 9, 13, 15–17, 43
    defined, 7
    land–capital, 8

regional, 6
religious, 3
Social Democratic Party, 45, 46, 57
Social identity model, 168–71
Staffordshire, 122
*Standard*, 36
Steed, Michael, 45, 52, 64, 73, 89
Stephen, Leslie, 29, 37
Stevenson, John, 46
Stewart, Marianne, 5
Stirlingshire, 115
Stokes, Donald, 6, 16, 65, 66, 84
Studlar, Donley, 2, 64, 67–70
Surrey, 115, 149, 151
Sussex, 141, 151
Sutherland, 29

Tanner, Duncan, 42
Test Acts (repeal of), 13
Thatcher, Margaret, 46, 93
Thatcherism, 80
Theories of voting,
    rational, 5–6, 70–5
    social identity models, 4, 66–70
Thompson, F. M. L., 19, 141
Thrift, Nigel, 141
Tiryakian, E. A., 78
Tithe Commutation Act (1836), 13, 32
Townsend, Alan, 177
Trade unions, 9

Transportation networks, as
    core–periphery indicator, 143–50
Travers, Tony, 46
Trevelyan, Charles, 39
Tufte, Edward, 71

Urwin, Derek, 10, 12, 78, 87, 92

Wade, L. L., 5, 73, 102
Wald, Kenneth, 3, 16, 33, 34, 104, 160
Wales
    and Conservative Party, 44
    and core–periphery placement, 87
    and Disestablishment of
        Established Church, 167
    devolution of power to, 174
    nationalism, 34–5, 84
Waller, Robert, 166
Ward, Hugh, 74
Watts, H. D., 117
Wellhofer, E. S., 9, 16, 32, 78, 82
Welsh Office, 177
West Yorkshire, 122
Westminster model, 65
Williams, Shirley, 45
Witherspoon, Sharon, 2, 67
Wrigley, E. A., 85, 140

Yorkshire, 89, 122, 141
Young, Lord, 1, 5